"In *Mom Connection,* Tracey Bianchi reaches up and unzips every mom's heart and makes us instantly friends with her. Real. Winsome. Approachable. Like us but still herself, Tracey convinces us we can connect. And once we realize we've connected with her, we're ready and prepared to connect with all the others in our lives."

—**Elisa Morgan**, president emerita, MOPS International; author, *She Did What She Could*

"Every mom knows that amidst its many blessings, the journey of motherhood brings its share of challenges. Tracey Bianchi understands what you are experiencing and provides comfort, candor, counsel, and companionship through the pages of this deeply encouraging book. Your heart, soul, and mind will be nourished and fed by Tracey's wit and wisdom, and after reading *Mom Connection*, you'll appreciate anew the essential truth that you need not travel this journey alone. Every mom I know should read this book!"

—**Helen Lee**, author, *The Missional Mom*; cofounder, Redbud Writers Guild

"Such intimacy and wisdom! This practical and fun read encourages moms everywhere—motherhood may not always be 'peppy bliss,' yet in the midst of it we find our unique groove by connecting with our own hearts, families, friends, and God."

—**Shayne Moore**, activist; author, *Global Soccer Mom*

"If you've ever felt alone as a mom, you must read this book! Reading it is like sitting down for coffee with a hip mentor mom (who still has preschoolers at home), and listening to her realistic, witty advice and authentic, fearless admission of her own insecurities and questions. Instead of just saying 'be yourself,' Tracey Bianchi says, 'You are not alone!' and offers specific ways to find friends and thrive as a mom. Her 'mom-tested tips' in each chapter are practical, doable, inspiring. She offers specific ways that we can trust ourselves (and God!) enough to find meaningful connections with others that will empower us as moms. Highly recommended!"

—**Keri Wyatt Kent**, MOPS speaker; author, *Deeper into the Word* and *Breathe*

mom connection

Creating Vibrant Relationships in the Midst of Motherhood

TRACEY BIANCHI

Revell
a division of Baker Publishing Group
Grand Rapids, Michigan

Published by Revell
a division of Baker Publishing Group
P.O. Box 6287, Grand Rapids, MI 49516-6287
www.revellbooks.com

Printed in the United States of America

Library of Congress Cataloging-in-Publication Data

Bianchi, Tracey, 1972–
Mom connection : creating vibrant relationships in the midst of motherhood / Tracey Bianchi.
p. cm.
Includes bibliographical references.
ISBN 978-0-8007-2115-2 (pbk.)
1. Motherhood. 2. Motherhood—Religious aspects—Christianity. 3. Mothers—Psychology. 4. Interpersonal relations. I. Title.
HQ759.B55 2012
306.874′3—dc23 2011051193

Published in association with the literary agency of Alive Communications, Inc., 7680 Goddard Street, Suite 200, Colorado Springs, Colorado 80920, www.alivecommunications.com.

To protect the privacy of those who have shared their stories with the author, some names and details have been changed.

12 13 14 15 16 17 18 7 6 5 4

For Traci—
your laughter is forever in our hearts.

And for the rest of the girls from
Alabama Avenue—
neighbors forever, sisters for always.

Contents

Section Three
Sharing Your Rhythm

Introduction

I totally text people while playing hide-and-seek with my kids. That, or try to sneak a two-minute nap. Lying in the bathtub, I hear echoes and shrieks rising through the floor. They are still downstairs. I close my eyes and try to breathe deep while plastic bath toys poke my lower back. Maybe I can fire off a text or two before they find me? I confess that I'm quickly bored and not one of those creative moms who truly cherishes playtime. I forget the name of my dolly. I lose patience searching for a Lego. As far as playmates go, I fear I am among the worst.

But whenever my kids bust out a vintage toy that takes me back to age eight, I'm all in. One of motherhood's hidden perks is the chance to relive our own playtime through our child's toys. Like the Fisher-Price Family Farm. Operation and Bristle Blocks make me squeal, and I nearly passed out when I found my old Cabbage Patch Kid in my parents' basement. Xavier Roberts would have been proud. When my oldest received Mouse Trap for his birthday, I was way more excited than he was. These games recall a time when play was effortless, when smiles came easy, and when the rhythm of my life mostly involved waking up, snacking, and playing.

Sure, the lure of memorabilia is strong, but beyond the fact that my old Strawberry Shortcake dolls still smell the same, these toys represent a time when playmates and free time came easy, when sunblock was optional but roller skates with tube socks were not. Relationships depended on your ability to stay out late and play kickball down the block.

Today I'm blessed to be a parent. Motherhood is both the greatest joy and ache my body and soul have ever known, and it comes with a different rhythm than playing Barbies on the driveway in June.

For example, on most days my children come utterly unglued sometime around 4:00 p.m. At 3:30 I brace myself for the persistent, whiney, "Is dinner ready yet?" drama that besieges us. Never mind the fact that I try in earnest to fend off the bedlam. I dish up perfectly balanced midday snacks that could be featured in *Parenting* and use my calm yet deliberate voice all afternoon. Like the Wicked Witch of the West, if I so much as utter the word "no" after 4:01, my kids melt into sassy little puddles, oozing attitude all over the kitchen floor.

I grit my teeth and lament our downfall, yet I also recognize their little bodies have a rhythm that dictates a need for food and rest at that hour. This same biological rhythm has them eagerly at my bedside by 6:00 a.m. hollering "Mama, get up, Mama, get up." By 8:00 a.m. their bodies have stockpiled so much energy that they spill out of the house like a bag of super balls. By 10:00 a.m. they need a snack. And on it goes.

You and I have rhythms as well. Our very bodies rely upon the beating of our hearts to keep up with our toddlers (roughly 100,000 beats per day). Our breathing is cadenced, and one reason we struggle with newborns is that our circadian rhythms suddenly flip. Up at night and yearning for sleep during the day, we feel more like nocturnal raccoons during those first weeks of life, with black circles under our eyes to match. It is also the very rhythm of labor and contractions that gives life to those babies.

Rhythm is our friend. Ask any athlete, dancer, musician, or cardiologist. Move too quickly or haphazardly and life becomes a truncated string of disjointed experiences. Moments we were designed to enjoy become just one more detail on a list to check off before hitting the pillow. Each of us has a unique, natural cadence we are called to live.

Our culture has hijacked many of our rhythms. We can shop online 24/7 and grow vegetables inside during February. Technology keeps those of us who work always connected to the office, leaving 9 to 5 just a nice idea from that old Dolly Parton movie. It's exhausting to be a parent in our generation.

Yet while our cell phones buzz and online deals beckon at midnight, our children call us to the innocent rhythms of being alive. Author and mother Dorothy Bass once wrote about her three-year-old daughter's awareness of time and rhythm. One morning she asked an apparently simple question. "Mommy, what time is it?" to which Bass offered a variety of clock-oriented options. None were satisfactory, so her frustrated child responded, "No, no. Halloween all finished, Christmas all finished, Valentine's all finished. What *time* is it?" Bass says, "There was an urgency in this question, an urgency even an adult could understand. If you don't know what time it is, you might miss something important: some fun, some stories, and lots of candy too."[1]

Learning to identify healthy life rhythms is important because they powerfully transform our parenting, our relationships, and our communities by giving us the space to settle into natural opportunities for connection. Author Adele Calhoun once offered this encouragement: "Go slowly for there is such little time."

This book is about living into life's rhythm so we can connect and create vibrant relationships as moms.

While the days of our own scooters and banana-seat bicycles have passed, we still swim in circles of potential playmates. The other women, mothers, friends, colleagues, and family members who surround our adult playgrounds each day. Navigating these relationships with integrity and discovering their rhythms will help us forge deeper connections.

The Hula Hoop

Of all the toys my memory can recall, the hula hoop is my favorite. A simple toy launched by the Wham-O corporation around 1957, it is a useless tube of plastic unless you step into the ring and whip up a little hip action. My friend Sonia gave me her old hula hoop to inspire this book, and I was reminded of both the effort and ease it took to keep that hoop spinning. How when the rhythm took over it looked like an episode of *Happy Days*, and it was fun. Thanks, Sonia!

Life of course is a bit more complicated, but ultimately we manage in a similar fashion. We step into the ring, hoist it up over our hips, and give it an earnest spin, hoping somehow our efforts will stick. If we find the right balance and cadence, which is so very doable for us moms, we may just thrive during motherhood. So will you join me for a conversation about what it takes to balance our lives and play vibrantly alongside one another? Will you come along to discover this is possible even at that 4:00 hour?

Section One

Why We Need Rhythm in Our Lives

1

Hula Hoops

Your Life Has a Rhythm

Life moves pretty fast—if you don't stop and look around, you could miss something.

—Ferris Bueller

The winner of the hoop race will be the first to realize her dream—not society's dream, her own personal dream.

—Barbara Bush

My Hot-Pink Hula Hoop

At age ten I received a hot-pink hula hoop, which garnered a considerable amount of my childhood attention. A perfect circle some 40 inches in diameter with a white pinstripe threaded around the tube, it was filled with gravel that added a soundtrack to my adventures. I would send it rolling across the lawn and cajole my younger sister into leaping through it like a dolphin. When she tired of my zoo tricks, I recruited a neighbor to play lion tamer. Later I had the unsuspecting boy across the street standing perfectly straight, a statue for my giant ring toss.

Eventually I actually learned how to hula with this hoop, and from the moment my hips embraced that rhythm I was pre-teen awesomeness. I raced through the neighborhood enlisting my girlfriends in hula hoop competitions. I even tried to outspin my mom, but she grew up in the 1950s so, whatever.

Did you know there are world records for hula hooping? The record for hula hooping with one hoop is seventy-two straight hours.[1] P.S.—There is also a world record for the man with the longest eyebrow in the world.

In January of 2009 the tremendously talented Australian Circus performer Jess Love claimed to trump all hula feats by swinging 115 hoops from her body for less than three seconds. In the video of her record-breaking feat, Jess arches her spine like a cat and from her center of gravity heaves a behemoth tower of hoops onto her back. Onlookers clap and cheer with fabulous Aussie accents. She stands perfectly still but her eyes betray the difficulty of this little maneuver, conjuring up a dramatic pause with 115 hoops pressing on her spine. Then in one sweeping movement, she flings the hoops left, sways her hips a few times, and lets 115 plastic circles drop to the ground. The crowd cheers.

Truth be told, the YouTube version[2] was quite anticlimactic, but apparently world record rules state that if all hoops make it to three full rotations, then you've got yourself a record. I kicked back in my chair after watching the Jess video. It was quiet in my house at that moment. Hockey gear sat piled at the back door, a renegade dirty diaper was wadded up next to the helmets and pads. My tired mind wondered if (and sort of hoped) the diaper would accidentally get scooped up and hauled to an ice arena. I spied a few crusty noodles from last Wednesday's dinner under the table. As an exhausted mother of three children under age seven, I thought Jess Love's three-second maneuver seemed a fitting metaphor for the world-record feats a mom pulls off daily.

Sometimes motherhood feels a little bit like twirling 100 hula hoops on a steaming hot sidewalk.

Child-Bearing Hips

A few decades later my days of slim hips scooting in circles have been replaced by well-padded mama hips that hold babies and diaper bags. And while the thought of hoisting even one hoop is mostly laughable, as moms we swing a world-record number of them each and every day. Tag it with whatever cliché you'd like—spinning plates, keeping those proverbial balls in the air, juggling or balancing acts, or my favorite, managing a three-ring circus. If you are a mom, you move in seemingly endless circles and keep a mind-boggling number of ideas, events, and commitments spinning every single day.

For the mother of a newborn infant, sleep is now just a craving that taunts us with little swigs of our formerly luscious eight uninterrupted hours. Feeding schedules, work, spouses or single-parent life, in-laws, and worry place seemingly untenable demands upon our bodies and our hijacked brains.

And every mom knows the day that baby learns to walk is enthralling for all of about an hour until our wobbly little person nearly pulls down a formerly benign bookcase, now potential death trap. As our children grow, the hoops keep flying at us: siblings, preschool schedules, our own career goals, considerations of adopting again. Pick your acronyms—PTA, PTO, an IEP, and eventually the ACT.

Author and speaker Julie Ann Barnhill once called motherhood "the guilt that keeps on giving." So add to the stack of hoops our dreams and hopes for our children and the nagging sense that we could mess this all up. The weight pressing on our spine intensifies.

Facebook, Twitter, email, and other media outlets add a few more time-consuming hoops, as does the co-worker struggling through her divorce, the aunt with cancer, the dream we dared to try to keep by taking a night class. If you have a child with special needs, you know the additional weight of particular classes, therapies, treatments, or appointments with physicians and specialists.

Before long we find ourselves slumped over on the sidewalk like a street performer, trying desperately to put on our best game face while hauling around the hulking stack of relationships and responsibilities that makes up our lives.

Inevitably the hoops crash to the pavement and we wonder why exactly it is that we are all-out screaming with our arms flying, frantic because a toddler spilled her bowl of crackers on the laptop. Maybe things are a bit out of rhythm?

A Different Way to Spin through Life

The standard complaint of our generation is that we are busy and stressed. Museums someday will describe us as the generation of Starbucks drive-thru's and minivans with more onboard entertainment options than a theater. It seems quite normal, funny, and even celebrated these days to feel like Helen Hunt in *Twister*—that scene when she and Bill Paxton are clinging to a railing while an entire barn gets ripped to pieces and swirls all around them.

This is hailed as normal.

We buy greeting cards that celebrate this sentiment.

We watch movies about it.

Some of us even write books about it.

A chilled-out, balanced mother is a complete anomaly.

Can you imagine for a moment if, when someone were to ask how you were doing, what it might feel like to answer by saying, "I'm actually doing quite well, not too stressed or busy." And what would you say if someone offered that reply? I'm not talking at all about perfection here, rather an ability to live purposefully within life's inescapable imperfections.

I love the title of Carla Barnhill's book *The Myth of the Perfect Mother* because it boldly states there is no such thing. Our generation of mothers gets this. We self-identify with it. The most wildly popular mommy blogs see thousands of visitors per day stopping by to agree with one another about the imperfect side of motherhood. I'm one of those bloggers and visitors, and I celebrate the adrenaline rush that comes from finding another woman who "totally understands my life." But beyond that celebrated moment, how do we move ahead? How exactly are we supposed to love and grow in this storm? Should frantic be the norm?

I'm a horribly slow runner. I should really define my activity as shuffling more than running. But I love the sport, I love the way it feels when my legs and lungs connect and my stride opens up. My breathing settles into place and I begin to feel like Flo Jo on a three-mile run. If you drove past me, you would see a clunky suburban mom jogging on the sidewalk, but in my soul, at that moment, I am a Kenyan Olympian. I consider it a good run if I find my rhythm, my groove. My exercise is nowhere near perfect, but when all the parts of my body are in sync and those endorphins kick in, I am unstoppable.

To Barnhill's point, the perfect mother does not exist, yet some women seem to hold tight in the tornado and emerge stronger, more thoughtful and purposeful than they were the day their first child came home. They do not strive for perfection, but as they shuffle down the sidewalk, they have indeed found their groove. They are in sync with their own souls and the desires of their hearts. They admit the challenges yet embrace the messiness. They live vibrant, connected lives because they have settled into a rhythm.

Another Hula Hoop Record

In 2010, Jin Linlin of China performed a hula hoop dance at the New Year's Peace Gala in Chicago. On a mostly dark stage with perfectly placed spotlights, she emerged with a glittery silver stack of 300 hula hoops.

A tiny woman, Jin Linlin walked powerfully toward center stage and, with arms perfectly poised and in a similar maneuver as Jess Love, she leaned slightly and heaved the stack of hoops onto her back in preparation to spin. She paused, then threw her lower body to the side and relinquished the hoops to the rhythm of her hips.

The crowd erupted as Jin Linlin's steady pulsed dance maintained height on all her hoops. After several seconds had passed, rather than dropping the hoops with a truncated thud, Jin's hoops began to spread and sway across her entire body. As Jin's hips oscillated from left to right, her stack of silver hoops unfurled up her torso to cover her arms and lift over her head, while the lower hoops slithered with ease toward the floor—all 300 spinning gorgeously the entire time.

Jin Linlin looked like a giant Slinky.

She had 300 moving parts that slipped together in one grace-filled cadence. The wider her hoops drifted from their center, the more inspiring her feat as she moved across the stage to thunderous applause.

Okay, now don't panic. I promise I am not about to suggest that you perfectly balance 300 tasks and relationships (again, Carla's wisdom). But there is a lesson here for our generation of overcommitted, overcaffeinated moms. We can jump the chaos ship anytime we want, celebrating the imperfections and forging new territory together.

Finding Your Groove

Of course, motherhood will eternally be a balancing act with bouts of stress and worry (even depression), a mixture of global concern and lost lunch boxes. I do not believe there is any one equation that works for everyone (and I bombed every math class, so I'd get the equation wrong anyway). But each one of us has a standing invitation to self-evaluation. How exactly do we want this whole motherhood thing to go down? Everyone claims this season races. I haven't blinked since my son was born. If I do I'm afraid he will suddenly be eighteen.

How do we want our families and friends to remember us?

And yes, even that niggling, super-morbid question . . .

What would they say about us at our funeral?

What will our legacy to them be?

Mom Connection will take you on a journey toward celebrating and discovering the underlying rhythm of your life and how that rhythm pulls you into vibrant relationships. I hope you will discover that your unique situation and the details of your mothering journey can be lived in freedom, opening up your life to relationships and transforming formerly lonely places. Gracefully engaging the people who cross your path rather than viewing them as tasks on a list. Investing in your community, fostering healthy marriages, and finding out that ultimately you are connected to a bigger dance.

Maybe this all sounds more than a little daunting to you at the moment. I confess it often feels that way to me. But our very lives depend on finding our groove, and most of us will discover burdens lifted and hearts opened in the process. We may discover a place that lies beyond a generation of celebrated chaos.

FIVE Mom-Tested Tips

Each chapter will end with five ideas to help you get started with the concepts discussed. This will be our rhythm together as readers. The first three tips will be practical ideas to try. The fourth will always be a prayer or blessing of some sort. The fifth, an idea to journal or write about. Consider grabbing a fancy-pants notebook to keep track of the prayers and questions. All are guilt-free ideas you can take or leave. The goal is to discover what works for you. These are mom-tested and hopefully helpful to you. Here are your "Mom-Tested Tips" from this chapter:

1. **Purchase a hula hoop.** Stand out in your backyard and enjoy a childlike indulgent moment to get a little rhythm going for your body and your heart. Can you recall an activity, sport, dance, or musical endeavor where you felt as though you had indeed found your groove? Motherhood, understandably, often shoves our former passions into the attic. Let the memories soak your mind again. Teach your kids about your hula hoop and how to swing it and sway.

2. **Remember your limits.** Kick back on your couch and take your pulse. Listen to your own breathing by slowing it down and spending at least a full minute on deep, intentional breaths—like yoga class. Remember you are a creature who lives because of rhythm. You cannot even breathe were it not for the very God-given rhythms of your own body. You are finite and limited; this

can be a tremendously freeing thought. Rest for a moment and consider all that is beyond your grasp. Enjoy the fact that even though life can feel heavy, it does not actually rest upon your little shoulders.

3. **Have a daily dance party.** Often I concede victory at the 4:00 hour and flip on good music—music I actually like—to get the grumpy energy out. You can all sway and spin like Beyoncé wannabes, then sit back and watch as every muscle in your children's bodies flail around. Watch them try to find their rhythm. Developmentally their efforts at finding a groove are disjointed, yet the sheer thrill of trying to catch the beat keeps them at it. Make it an ethereal moment for yourself as you consider how much fun they have just trying to find their rhythm. Can life really be that easy?

4. **Pray.** Even if you are not sure what you believe about God, take a moment at the end of each day and pray for a healthy rhythm in your life. Think about one desire you hold for your children or your community and ask God to show you the way to make space for that dream. It can take less than one minute to pray, and a fancy theological vocabulary is not a prerequisite. For example, "God, please help me find the way through my life, help me live well in the time and space you've given me."

5. **Journal.** Spend time briefly writing out the emotions connected with your weekly routine. Take a look at the last seven days and write out what the

bright spots and the places of struggle were. Is there a lonely time in your day? Are you not able to sleep well (for reasons beyond a newborn)? Do you rely on adrenaline or caffeine to power through your afternoon? Where are joy-filled moments? Lunchtime with your kids? A meeting with your colleague? When do you find time to exercise? Answer these questions and look at how time ebbs and flows for you. Where are the smiles and sorrows? This will help craft a reference point to the conversations in this book.

Thumbs UP Thumbs DOWN

Also at the end of each chapter, we will take a little space to reflect together. What is one idea from the chapter that you would consider trying with your family or friends? And what is one idea that does not fit into your idea of rhythm at all, and why? Consider reviewing these two questions with a small group, your MOPS table, a good friend, or even your spouse.

How does the idea of living into a better rhythm excite and motivate me?

____

____

____

How does this idea of living into a rhythm make me nervous or feel uncertain?

____

____

____

BOOKS, PEOPLE, and OTHER RANDOM STUFF

Finally, each chapter will end with some resources, movies, websites, and organizations that may help you connect further with this conversation. For example:

- YouTube view of Jin Linlin's hula hoop feat (one minute in), http://www.youtube.com/watch?v=NiQaDgj8Z10
- Richard Foster, *Freedom of Simplicity: Finding Harmony in a Complex World*
- Adele Calhoun, *Spiritual Disciplines Handbook: Practices That Transform Us*
- Katrina Kenison's blog, *The Gift of an Ordinary Day,* http://www.katrinakenison.com/
- Books and resources by Dr. Archibald Hart (researcher and psychologist with much to say about adrenaline, stress, depression, and the pace of our lives)

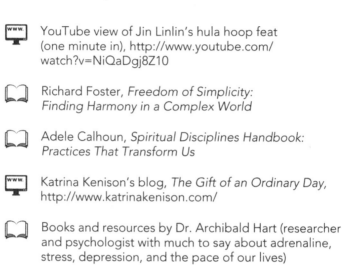

2

Teeter-Totter

Moving beyond Competition to Connection

Friendship is born at that moment when one person says to another, "What! You too? I thought I was the only one."

—C. S. Lewis

She thinks she's going to have a party and not invite me?

—Regina George from *Mean Girls*

Born to Be a Mom (or Not)

I've always been a fan of graceful women, whether Audrey Hepburn, Coco Chanel, or even Gwyneth Paltrow and the way she holds herself at the Oscars. I admire the elegant choreography of life, like the way Cinderella glided into her glass slipper. A demure, silky maneuver that revealed her poise and finesse. There are many women I know whose journey into motherhood is flowing with this same natural agility. Women who slide into motherhood like a glass slipper.

Their bodies respond perfectly to pregnancy as if incubating a seven-pound child was second nature, like chewing. Nursing is a breeze. They operate so smoothly that birthing and chasing children appear to be old routines, and of course they slide into pre-pregnancy jeans four weeks post-pregnancy. These are the moms who can offer up an unforced smile just one week into life with a newborn. "How does she do it all?" we ask.

Natural Moms, I call them. I am super jealous.

Motherhood smacked me upside the head. Truly. After a perfectly planned pregnancy, I expected nothing but postpartum bliss. Sure, a few sleepless nights, but I thought motherhood would be like the cover of a Pottery Barn Kids catalog, all pink lemonade and green gingham.

I've never been one for grace and elegance. My mother has urged me to sit up straight since elementary school. I took one ballet class but was the chubby kid who could not properly manage an arabesque, so I got stuck in the back row. It is awesome to stuff a pouchy tummy into a periwinkle spandex leotard. My life is less like Cinderella and more like her cloddy stepsisters trying to wedge their fat feet into posh footwear. So why exactly was I shocked when my parenting plan went awry?

I'd arranged for an earthy midwife and natural delivery. What I got was twenty-four hours of labor, Pitocin, stitches, and one glorious epidural before giving birth to my firstborn son. Instead of savoring the moment with our granola midwife, my husband and I had monitors, machines, a neonatologist, a baby all tangled up in his cords, and two MDs. When the flurry of activity had subsided, I sat shocked and literally numb, staring blankly at my child.

We snapped pictures. We took footprints.

Then I went home and cried for hours.

Every day.

For six weeks straight. Six weeks.

Not a graceful moment in sight.

If my son Charlie wasn't eating, he was beet red, bleating like a newborn calf, screaming and writhing in pain. They told us he was "colicky," which is pediatrician-speak for "your life is going to suck for at least eight weeks." Walking, bouncing, crying, fighting. This was our everyday life. We could not go out for lunch or visit friends, for my child screamed nonstop until he passed out from exhaustion, at which point I did the same.

Both of us, with red puffy faces, just glared at one another with skepticism and pain.

Ah, motherhood.

The Park

The local park quickly became our sanctuary. My son did not stop crying when we ventured outside, but the passing cars at least muted his squeals. The breeze and vitamin D soothed my tired soul. There was hope outside, so we would trudge to the park and do a few laps until plopping onto a bench to watch the other moms.

I imagined their lives—what time they ate dinner, what parenting style worked for them, and how soon they potty-trained their youngest. Was she going back to work? My mind would then deftly slide into dangerous places, like curiosity over how she got so thin after having two kids, how she could afford to let her daughter play in such expensive shoes. And I would wonder why those three moms seemed such good friends. How could they be laughing during such an exhausting season of life? What did they have in common that bonded them so?

And why was I alone on a park bench? Where were *my* mommy friends? Could anyone feel my isolation?

A Familiar Feeling

Women in general, especially mothers, often feel this desperation.

Jen—my friend with two teenagers, two preschoolers, and an adopted special needs daughter—said her days at the park were spent "feeling alone, checking out the other moms, wondering how they have it all put together. Why they have friends and I do not. How painful it is to start conversations with other moms and then this fear—once you ask them a question, what will you say next?"

Courtney, a working mother of two, said, "My loneliness often stemmed from the fact that many of the women I first met didn't seem to want to make new friends—they just didn't have the time or energy to invest in anyone outside of their existing circle."

An old neighbor once lamented to me that she found motherhood to be the most isolating experience of her entire life.

Fear and loneliness. Have you ever wished they covered that in prenatal class?

As days merged into months, my son and I viewed one another with less skepticism and more empathy. We even cracked a few smiles. Our lives slowly morphed together like an old, worn jigsaw puzzle. The kind you discover on the bottom shelf at preschool. Tired pieces with thick frayed edges that betray a history of trying to fit together and landing in the wrong place. But eventually we snapped together.

Yet I was still longing for friendship. I knew connections were possible and that caring women to do motherhood with were out there. After all, I was not the first mother to grace planet Earth. But how could I—weepy, clingy, lucky-to-scrounge-up-time-for-a-shower, me—find them? And how would I ever make time for friendship with all the hoops I was already spinning? Nap schedules, part-time work, managing life at home, marriage, my own extended family. The heaps of poop-stained Onesies.

"Hello, My Name Is . . ."

I continued to amble to the park day after day and each time my insecurities mounted. I'd hear shrieks of laughter a few blocks over, clearly a pack of kids and parents who were friends. I'd watch bikes and Big Wheels zip past ahead of chatty, coffee-sipping parents plotting together about an upcoming vacation. I eavesdropped like the CIA.

"Just say hi to one of them," I'd tell myself. How hard can conversation be? "Comment on her stroller or ask about her dog." (Yes, I am this loser-ish).

Impossible.

Life often traps us in middle school. Rosalind Wiseman, author of *Queen Bees and Wannabes: Helping Your Daughter Survive Cliques, Gossip, Boyfriends, and the New Realities of Girl World*, explains that the social struggles that plague girls today linger long after high school is over.

Like maybe even, years later, when they follow us to the park with a newborn.

Fear of acceptance or rejection.

Competition.

The need to appear indifferent and resilient.

The desire to sit at the best lunch table with the trendy kids.

Turns out motherhood can dish up the same drama. Sure, we are older and supposedly wiser, but have you ever found yourself nervous about approaching another mom for conversation? Ever hesitated to host a playdate in your disorganized house or to drive the carpool in your messy van where chicken nuggets have established small villages under the seats?

Why?

As women, our culture has us locked into eternal competition at very young ages. From *America's Next Top Model* to Martha Stewart, underlying mantras of perfection garnish our days. And can we all agree that June Cleaver threw us under the bus?

Motherhood, rather than calming our fears, launches us into an entirely new arena of competition. One of the mentor moms at my MOPS group (in her fifties) once said to me, "I feel sorry for you girls these days—not only do you have all the old baggage of keeping up that we once did, you have to still look hot too."

How do I measure up?

Even though I am a mom, do I look too mom-ish?

Is my child keeping up?

Have we met all the designated milestones?

Are we in the right preschool or programs?

Have we been doing gymnastics since the womb in order to make the US Olympic team?

Let's pile on a few hoops, shall we?

A good friend, while nursing her newborn, once asked me, "Do I look like I know what I am doing? Like I deserve to be a mom?" We want to look like we can manage. We are wired for relationship and connection and yet are pitted against one another. Our educational systems rank us, our socioeconomic status can cripple us. Our labels precede us.

Labels like "single mom," "working mom," "at-home mom," and "military mom" identify our realities but can also leave us unfairly isolated. Children with special needs or unique situations bring life-changing questions to the table that are often misunderstood or flat-out ignored. Terms like "older mom," "teen mother," "blended family," or "adoptive mom" fly around our social circles, often landing with a sting.

Most of us know the heartache that comes from careless assumptions, judged for what appears as truth rather than the honest reality of our very hearts and souls. And yet we still crave connection. That is good news! The very design of our lives is to be together in life-giving relational circles. To find a daily rhythm that makes space for others is one consistent cry of a mother's heart.

We do not have to compete.

We can rally together with our pile of imperfections.

We can celebrate the march of time.

We can bond over messy houses and stretch marks.

Together, we can mock Snooki and the lack of any reality on TV.

Never Alone Yet Lonely

Motherhood, while marketed as a life stage of peppy bliss, can produce tremendous anxiety and isolation all, interestingly enough, while a woman is not physically alone. As moms we have little people literally hanging on us all day. We sleep with kids, nurse kids, strap kids to our chests in kangaroo-like carriers. We cannot leave the house, the car, the restroom without them. We are never physically alone and yet our souls starve for connection.

Often our best efforts at connection can be hijacked. Perhaps we finally make plans to connect with a new friend, only to wake up to a toddler with a fever of 102.9. Your poor pediatrician has just become the conversational high point of your day.

Competition. Labels. Cultural barriers. Physical limitations. Life stage obstacles. These prevent us from engaging with meaningful friendship circles every day. Is it any wonder that many sociologists and psychologists have declared an epidemic of loneliness in our culture? In 2008 the *Today Show* reported some 96 percent of moms today felt more stressed than their own mothers were.[1] According to research by the YMCA of the USA and the Abundant Assets Alliance, 53 percent of parents say they do not regularly seek support or parenting advice from friends, family, or the community. Umm . . . that's over half of all parents going it alone! Fears of appearing weak or needy prevent parents from reaching out for help, so they make major decisions and often parent in isolation.[2]

Hearing the Cry of a Mother's Heart

Back to the graceful, natural mothers . . . no amount of balance, wisdom, or insight can shape a perfect mother. Everyone struggles. We should find this tremendously freeing because it helps to know we do not struggle alone. The old cliché "misery loves company" applies.

At this life stage where emotions feel crisp and near crumbling, even a simple invitation can shape our days and weeks. Author Adele Calhoun says, "Invitations challenge and remake us. They can erode and devastate. And they can heal and restore us. Being wanted, welcomed, invited and included are some of the most mending experiences on the planet."[3]

So, it appears there is no woman at the park who is perfectly beyond the reaches of friendship, no woman who could not use a warm, genuine invitation. Opportunities to connect and encourage one another abound, for there is no label that is permanently affixed. We are on the same botched, imperfect, sometimes losing team. And the joy here is that the bench is filled with women like us. From the seemingly elegant to the obviously clunky, our shared yearnings and basic needs as mothers connect us.

Just like Christine (working mom of two who struggled to have children) said, "So many, many years I wanted a baby, and a daughter at that, and when I got her I was so certain I was going to be the mom who got it right—I would have motherhood down. And when it didn't go that way, I didn't know what to do!" She went on to say that because of the friendship and support of other moms, she is finally finding her way.

We are not on that park bench alone. Dare to believe this. You are not alone.

FIVE Mom-Tested Tips

1. **Read Dorothy C. Bass.** She wrote a great book called *Receiving the Day: Christian Practices for Opening the Gift of Time*, and in it you will find a great discussion about life and the rhythms we live. Consider picking up a copy and reading it with a few other moms or a small group. Bass will have you rethinking the sense of urgency we feel in our culture today and will help you dwell well where it matters.

2. **Stalk someone.** Well, not really, but scope out another mom who looks a little lonely on that park bench and consider plopping down next to her. Or, if you are that lonely mom, keep your eye on a woman you might consider approaching, say hello to her. Think about whether or not you might take a risk and engage her in conversation. Remember that her house is not perfect, her children are messy, and there is a pretty good chance she's had a few lonely moments along the way too. She probably does not know you are struggling either.

3. **Be present.** Next time you find yourself frustrated by a mom who appears distracted, uncaring, or simply oblivious, stop for a moment and remember that she is in the thick of it just like you. Maybe her grocery cart is in your way because she hasn't slept in three weeks. Maybe they just moved and her kid pushed yours and did not

apologize because the stress of setting up shop someplace new has them all exhausted. Give an abundant measure of grace and try to be present to the deeper realities behind another mom's actions, because there is always more to the story. It takes less than a minute to pause, breathe deep, and say to yourself, "Extend a little grace here."

4. **Pray.** Consider one of two prayers. Ask God simply and humbly to make you, as St. Francis once said, "an instrument of peace." Pray that you would be a blessing to others, pray for eyes to see the needs of women around you. Or pray for connection and friendship, for someone to extend the gift of companionship to you. Ask God to keep your heart open to this gift of others.

5. **Journal.** Recall a moment when you received love not because of your accomplishments or appearances but simply because someone noticed the good heart beating in your chest. Perhaps an old childhood friend, an encouraging teacher, parent, spouse, or your own child pointed out something simple yet poignant that nudged your soul. Like the time my daughter told me the lines (a.k.a. wrinkles) around my eyes made me look pretty. Or the fact that my own father still grins from ear to ear whenever I walk into the room. Journal a few thoughts on this acceptance. Fall asleep one night thinking about it. Recall the depths of that joy for a while and camp out there in your mind.

Thumbs UP Thumbs DOWN

What idea do you hope to put into practice for your family?

What does not work for your rhythm and why?

BOOKS, PEOPLE, and OTHER RANDOM STUFF

- Dee Brestin, *The Friendships of Women*
- Rosalind Wiseman: Creating Cultures of Dignity, http://rosalindwiseman.com
- David Benner, *The Gift of Being Yourself: The Sacred Call to Self-Discovery*
- Keri Wyatt Kent, *Breathe: Creating Space for God in a Hectic Life*

3

Two or More Players

We All Need Help

All I'm saying is, kindness don't have no boundaries.

—Kathryn Stockett from *The Help*

As Jesus and his disciples were on their way, he came to a village where a woman named Martha opened her home to him. She had a sister called Mary, who sat at the Lord's feet listening to what he said. But Martha was distracted by all the preparations that had to be made. She came to him and asked, "Lord, don't you care that my sister has left me to do the work by myself? Tell her to help me!"

—Luke 10:38–40

Nana

My own mother believes that I am an absolute catastrophe. She honestly winces and braces herself when she walks through my back door. Nana is amazing and loves us all deeply, but she's also a bit like a can of Mountain Dew that's been shaken up by a seventh grader yet remains unopened. She bites her "mother knows best" tongue, but I can tell she's bubbling up, just waiting for someone to crack that tab and burst with commentary on my life.

On the days she drops by for a visit, I hear the signature swoosh and thud of my back patio door announcing her arrival. I holler to the kids, "Nana's here!" And they come tumbling down the stairs cheering her name. Typically someone gets tangled in the mad rush and falls, lamenting the injustice of being tripped by a sibling before they even see my mother.

All this hullabaloo descends before my mom fully enters our house. The fact that Nana also has a crush on the dollar bin at Target does not help manage the activity level. Before her shoes are off, my trio is asking, "What'd ya bring us?" At this point she is digging through a plastic bag while still sporting her sunglasses. Someone is also still crying.

Before she gets settled in, I forget for a few moments that she's their Nana because she is also my mama and one of my deepest friends, so I start in on the latest news. What friend is pregnant, who is moving, why I wish I was ten pounds lighter, or how crazy it is at work lately. Everyone's camped out on the doormat.

She finally takes her coat off as I toss her a diet Coke and put on my own shoes. I'm usually headed out for errands when she stops by. It's like the most glorious dream in the world just to ride alone in my car. I can hardly wait to get out the door so I rattle off who needs what: "socks, mac'n'cheese, pick up at 3:00, baby, nap, almost out of milk."

Nana nods, drawing in a deep breath as I yank open that same sliding door, then she grabs my arm. "Honey, slow down." These have been her parting words to me for well over a decade. "Slow down. Take your time. Ask for help. Read my lips, slow down."

"Yeah, yeah, Ma, I got it. I know. Slow down. Ask for help. Okay. I'll be home by 4:00." Nana's advice is winsome, but the momentum of my life is fierce.

"Get 'er done"

The little quip "Get 'er done" (thank you, Larry the Cable Guy) fits my frenzy better than Nana's "slow down" line. You already know that mothers today face more fragmented demands on their time and energy than parents in any other era of US history. Many families find themselves harried and overprogrammed. Research suggests that parents today sign children up for a record number of activities. Not exactly a news flash.

The days when children would roam the neighborhood building backyard forts are disappearing. This is the era of AYSO, youth baseball, Mandarin lessons, and enrichment classes; a time when piano lessons, packed schedules, and understandable paranoia about safety keeps our kids inside or on a practice field. Which keeps parents shuttling them around in a minivan.

If we are not careful, our inner dialogue throughout the day will be to simply "get 'er done," whether laundry, dance class, meetings, or other work. I feel forever behind yet somehow give myself the grand illusion that maybe if I move quick enough I can indeed get it all done.

"Eventually I will catch up." Sure, of course you will . . .

Finding Freedom in the Daily Grind

So what's the solution? Pull your family off the grid? Maybe try life *Little House on the Prairie* style? "But if we drop traveling soccer now, she won't get to play in high school." We know the tension, but how can we trump it?

One of the best ways forward, and a tremendous source of joy, is to discover that sandwiched in the cracks of these routines and schedules lie everyday opportunities to build relationships and connections. We often promise ourselves connection time once we get it done. But what if we also connected *while* we were getting it done? By finding ways to slow it all down a bit yet remaining honest to the routines we keep? A MOPS speaker from Union Chapel in Muncie, Indiana, once simply said about life, "Sometimes it's hard because it's hard." My favorite magnet on our fridge says "It's so involved being me."[1] Every day demands attention to so many details. Yet every day is also a chance to connect with others within those demands.

This is a tipping point that might take our generation one step farther on the journey. If we all agree that parenting is hectic, then what is the next step? After that initial moment where we commiserate on the chaos, how does the camaraderie continue? Our routines are brimming with opportunities to spill love into the lives of others. We just have to take a step back and reevaluate.

Task lists do not have to be barriers to relationships; instead they can be the very source of our connections. If I keep telling myself that I'll call a certain friend or forge a special connection once things slow down a bit, the reality is that it may be a very long time before that happens. Perhaps calling that particular person is what it will take to actually slow down!

The Connections of Women

For centuries women have bonded together in their work. Often forced into specific roles or intentionally separated from mainstream society, they received opportunities to deepen their connections. History is rich with stories of sisters and friends, mothers and daughters who stood hip to hip everywhere from the kitchen sink to the birthing room.

During the Tudor Era (English Monarchy 1400–1600s), pregnant women of nobility would spend the final weeks of their pregnancies in confinement. Women would be removed from the presence of men and be attended only by midwives, friends, and their ladies in waiting. These women were to help prepare for birth, and comfort, encourage, and support the expecting mother. Childbirth was a mysterious world that men did not have the understanding or stomach to enter, so women would spend weeks and sometimes months together awaiting the birth of a child—telling stories, mending, sewing, connecting, bringing forth new life.

My own mother, my aunt Lil, my sister, and I spent years side by side at the kitchen sink on Christmas Day. The menfolk (as my mother jokingly called them) would retire to the living room to rub their bellies and moan, wishing they'd skipped the jello mold. Meanwhile, the four of us would slosh soapy dishes around in the sink and catch up on life. I'd suppress my feminist leanings long enough to embrace the opportunity for alone time with my sister and aunt. Elbow-deep in suds, we'd laugh, scrub pots and pans together, and tell stories of elusive cousins, bizarre relatives, and people we missed.

I see yet another relational community play out weekly in my local coffee shop. If I pop in for caffeine after our preschool drop-off, the place is jammed with moms and strollers. Women sporting T-shirts and ponytails fretting over sippy cups and Goldfish crackers fill almost every table. Standing in line, I totally eavesdrop on conversations that range from which teacher is the kindest to which mom is heading to work later that afternoon. I watch as toddlers shove aside a few stray professionals while grabbing at the juice boxes in the display case. It's all estrogen from 8:30 to 10:00 a.m.

These are places to find a few partners for the journey.

Laundry at 2:00 a.m.

My precious friend Amy's life offers notes from the pages of a mom who is finding freedom in her routine. She can function as a mother of four on the same sort of sleep schedule I could only manage at age eighteen. Every week I chat it up with her on a day she was awake until 2:00 a.m. working. Did I mention that she squeaked out all four of those children in just five years, they are all under eight, and one is a daughter with special needs?

Amy's a mess (she would totally agree, I'm not being mean). But she's a beautiful mess. She offers me one of the deepest friendships my soul has ever known. Amy will be the first to tell you her life is a debacle and she is up to her headband in missing socks, casseroles, karate, basketball, reading, laundry. Last time we chatted, her daughter Elizabeth (age two) had successfully knocked out a tooth and colored her face with blue marker. All in a day's work.

Amy is under no false illusion that her life will ever ease up, so she found a little peace and space in her schedule by choosing to do her laundry in the middle of the night.

She often catches me up on new thoughts and ideas that came to her while folding sheets at 1:30 a.m. She brushes up on music and pop culture while her family sleeps. She's been known to fire off the most sappy emails of love and friendship at 3:30 a.m. Not every night of course, just when the laundry pile could potentially ingest two of her kids.

Amy will tell you she's completely exhausted yet looks forward to a night when the house is quiet and she can finally ruminate on a few ideas. For her this time is a tremendous source of connection to others. It's when she does her best thinking, and while the rest of her mommy comrades are asleep, she thinks of and prays for them too. It's the very rhythm of her work that helps her connect with women in the same life stage.

Understandably, not all of us (or really hardly any of us) will find our groove at 2:00 a.m. But Amy gives a glimpse of what is possible when we discover our own unique rhythm. Regardless of the time of day or night, we must find some margin in our routine that opens us up to reflect a bit and connect. Uncovering new places in your schedule to chat, ponder, sing, email, write, or offer encouragement to others is one great way to manage the daily details and remain in sync with the people who matter most to you.

Finding Your Own Space

Creating a wider margin in your routine does not require you to sign up for another class or carve out time that does not currently exist. It simply asks that you view the daily grind differently by looking for places to bring what seem like disjointed duties into a life-giving rhythm.

Here's an easy example. Whenever we pile into our car after an outing, after the last seat belt is buckled, I shut the car doors and take my time walking around to the driver's side. The car is usually rocking a bit, I can hear muffled shrieks and snack requests through the window, so as I walk toward my door I intentionally slow down (except, of course, when it is

104 degrees outside). It's like a mini-spa for my mind. I take a deep breath, stand at the tailgate, and roll my neck around a few times, loving the fact that no one is hanging on me.

I pause.

I crunch and release my shoulders one last time.

I hop back in.

Less than thirty seconds later my mind is rested.

Mealtime Madness

You can also increase your margin by identifying where you struggle the most with your daily routine. Confess your inadequacies to others. Squeak out details of where you struggle. One woman's struggle is often another's triumph.

My issues are from 4:00 to 6:00 p.m. Can I get an amen? My friend Rhonda once said, "I'm having a good day if I don't yell at them by 9:00 a.m." So, by 4:00 p.m. most of us have yelled more than we planned. We have our recurring tough spots. Before I was a parent, I would hear moms and dads moan about the dinner hour. "Sheesh, what's the big deal?" I would naively quip.

Then came this phase of life when my elementary school child walks through the door as surly as a sailor crabbing for crackers, complaining that everyone is too loud for him. First grade is apparently quite stressful. On any given day as the clock ticks past 4:00, my toddler begins to holler for snacks and randomly throws her sippy cup. Meanwhile, my normally amicable four-year-old suddenly freaks out if you even look at him.

I trip over piles of shoes while trying to find homework sheets. My baby girl poops and I keep saying, "Don't worry, Mama will change you." And then forget instantly that she needs a diaper as I yank pots and pans out of cupboards and wish that

I had paid some attention to Rachael Ray. What's for dinner? Day-old quesadillas and yogurt cry out to me from the fridge.

While cajoling my oldest to broaden his culinary horizons (say, like by eating even chicken), my daughter waltzes through the kitchen smelling like a summer breeze near a pig farm and I remember that diaper. It's almost 5:00 p.m.

Whipping up dinner makes me an anxious, hot mess, and if the doorbell or phone rings, I normally cringe and ignore it. But often that ring is a woman just in the throes of her own dinnertime coup. Sometimes the most soul-shaping idea is to turn off the mac'n'cheese and stand on the lawn yucking it up with the neighbor.

Nia (blended family with four kiddos) shared a story of calling another mom during her dinner frenzy. A two-minute question turned into a thirty-two-minute conversation. Both moms overlooked the perfect meal and yammered away because they needed conversation to survive.

I've let my children snarf down chicken nuggets on the front porch so they can cruise the sidewalk with neighbor kids as I chat it up after a long day. At times the best way to manage is by sneaking away from the predetermined schedule.

Perhaps rather than trump the chaos we can redirect it? Will dinner with toddlers ever be easy? So why pretend? In the summer we often eat dinner at our community pool. Swim a bit and have hot pretzels and soda with other kids. Nutritional benefit = 0. But you get the point. Chaos will not disappear at this life stage, but we can change how we face it.

Dial up another mom at dinnertime and see what happens.

"I'd Ask for Help, But . . ."

Help. That four-letter word offers up a confession of inadequacy. "No, no, it's okay, I'm good. I've got this." Mmm-hmm, yeah right. I'm not afraid to admit my disaster-ness. Most of us are probably beyond that hang-up. What I love about our generation of mothers is that we are pretty open about our struggles. Yet, we still rarely ask for help. My catch is that I don't want to be the needy friend/mom because I don't want to burden you and definitely don't want to have to owe you—which is pretty much ridiculous as most of us do not keep score. It's easier to be the giver of help. So I suck it up and forge ahead.

I'd much rather have you drop your kids at my house, would rather drive the carpool or bring you a meal. Let me help you. When we help others, it strangely places us in a position of power (which sounds super narcissistic, but hang with me for a bit). I'm not suggesting that we help so that we can sit up a notch from our friends. But there are subtle nuances to asking for help that prick the soul—subtleties that consciously or subconsciously prevent us from asking others to lend a hand.

If I ask you to help me, then do I owe you?

Are you strangely in a position of power?

Will you think I am terrible if I cannot return the favor?

Will you think I am too needy?

Here's the catch. By refusing to ask for help, we rob others of the joy and privilege that come from lending a hand. We steal an opportunity for them to give what they have, to open their doors and hearts. We hog all the opportunity. Sometimes asking for help is just as good for the giver as it is for the asker. Sometimes asking for help is, well, helping.

So ask for it.

Confessions Get You Great Ideas for Dinner

My working-mom friend Tricia had the guts to go public with her culinary shortcomings. "At a mom's night out I sheepishly admitted that I only knew how to cook a total of three dishes. After my friends picked up their jaws from the floor, they immediately rallied to tell me about their most fail-safe recipes. I had over thirty recipes emailed to me within a week of my confession and have been using them ever since!" Tricia went on to say that "we all have things we need to rely on others for and that is where the gift of community shines the brightest."

I'm able to type this very chapter because my friend Robin five blocks over took one look at my panicky face and said, "I'm kidnapping your kids on Friday morning so you can go write." The "I can do it all and don't need anyone's help" part of me immediately said, "Nah, it's okay, I can get it all done."

"Seriously?! You are such a liar," she said.

On Friday I dropped them off at her doorstep.

Social Media to the Rescue?

Lisa attends a MOPS group that encouraged members to ask for help from one another via Facebook. The first post started with a request from the coordinator to confess one thing they all need help with, then she dared someone to go first. It started out slowly, but once a few moms cracked by laying out their needs the momentum shifted and relationships grew. Within a few hours women were offering to help one another plant flower gardens, do laundry, organize, and clean up clutter.

One beautiful part of this Facebook thread was noticing how everyone had a need as well as something to offer. Tips on meal planning, organization, gardening, and working that might normally be cloistered in our heads and homes became an amazing gateway to help another mom. Sometimes we can connect by leaning on some of the technology available to us.

If it feels safe (as in that shady guy you dated for one week in high school is NOT a Facebook friend) and you are comfortable enough with the technology, there are amazing avenues to receive rapid feedback, tips, help, and advice. Consider tossing out ideas and pleas for help on Twitter, Facebook, Google+, or a blog.

Just for grins I tossed up a Facebook question asking for good ways to rest and relax. Thirty-eight ideas, opinions, and heartfelt comments in thirty-six hours. The only catch is making sure you do not let Facebook suck away your life (I just spent one full hour on Facebook when all I was after was this thirty-second fact).

So Take the Risk

Creak open the front door or pick up the phone and find out that most moms share the same stresses and fears. If we can celebrate all that is good and joy-filled from this stage, and confess where we struggle, we might triumph over some of our isolation and begin to really swing in rhythm together. And if we dare to ask for help, these relationships move even deeper, for suddenly we have a purpose together. We are both blessed to give and to receive. We are standing on the front lawn with a hot-pink hula hoop and it's dinnertime and we are late for basketball practice, yet none of that even matters because we just keep asking the whole block to come outside and play.

FIVE Mom-Tested Tips

1. **Put hurry on a sabbatical.** Jean Blackmer offers a great idea in her book *MomSense.* Try for one whole day not to say the words "hurry up" (or any version thereof). Letting your children set the pace for your day will force you to live into the rhythm of their lives.[2] This will definitely slow you down! I tried this for a day and by noon nearly bit off my tongue. But we survived and it was a lovely day, less arguing, we missed a few appointments along the way but made up for it with better time together. Put hurry on a sabbatical for a day.

2. **Go slowly.** If #1 sounds appealing, try taking it a step further. Stretch out your day by slowing down and you may notice new places to connect along the way. Intentionally dawdle or drive in the right lane. Chew your food more slowly at dinner or take a few extra moments to just sit on the edge of your bed and draw in some deep breaths before your feet hit the floor and your day begins. Try five long breaths before hopping out of bed in the morning.

3. **Dinner on the front lawn.** Skip the formal dinner plans one night and dine on the front lawn, sidewalk, or balcony. Intentionally put yourself out where others roam so you can chat a bit during your regular routine. Maybe one of your neighbors will even join you. Lay out a blanket

and make it a picnic, bake a pan of brownies, or pick up a pile of cookies at the store so folks can share your dessert. And if no one stops by, at least you won't have to sweep the kitchen floor after dinner. Crumbs on the lawn!

4. **Prayer.** If we struggle to ask others for help, let's at least try to ask God for help. That seems an easy idea when big life-moments happen and we suddenly find ourselves on our knees. But what about with the daily routine? Craft a few prayers in your heart that give you the space to ask God for help with the things that perhaps no one else knows about. "God, help me not cry today." Or, "God, please calm my nerves as I am heading back to work." Or simply, "God, you've got my back, right? Please?"

5. **Journal.** I owe Jean Blackmer again for this one. Take a day and write a timeline of where your time and efforts go. Sort of like if you have ever counted calories on a diet and now you realize how many calories come from those M&M's you popped into your mouth throughout the day. Just list your routine for a day and then journal about the following:

   - Looking back over this day, what was the overarching feeling about this day? Harried? Sad? Tired? Rested? Joyful?

   - What triggers that emotion? Was it the amount of time you spent in the car or the fact that you had time to walk? Notice the connection between your general state of mind at the end of the day and how your time was spent. If you could draw a pie chart of how you spent your time, what would it reveal about your day? Take a moment to journal a few thoughts about your use of time and your mental health.

Thumbs UP **Thumbs DOWN**

Where can you find connection in your chaos?

Where do you find this idea impossible?

BOOKS, PEOPLE, and OTHER RANDOM STUFF

- Ann Kroeker, *Not So Fast: Slow-Down Solutions for Frenzied Families*
- Elisabeth Corcoran, *Calm in My Chaos: Encouragement for a Mom's Weary Soul*
- The Practicing Our Faith project, with many great ideas and conversations, http://www.practicingourfaith.org/
- Vicki Abeles's documentary film, *Race to Nowhere,* http://www.racetonowhere.com
- Dr. Daniel D. Meyer's *Living inSANITY* sermon series. Download it here from the Christ Church of Oak Brook Media Library, http://www.cc-ob.tv/search.php?series_id=47&category=Sermon

4

Hide-and-Seek

Discovering Your Gifts and Talents

A man may work from dawn to setting sun, but a woman's work is never done.

—English proverb

Talent is like electricity. We don't understand electricity. We use it.

—Maya Angelou

Real Men Sew

My husband Joel does all the sewing and mending in our home. He's an engineer by trade and the sort of linear thinker who can rebuild a Honda engine without furrowing a brow. So, over the years when I've found myself exasperated by a broken zipper or Cub Scout patch, he busts out the sewing machine my grandma Patzem handed down and I cheer. I cannot thread the darn thing and have no idea how to wind a bobbin. He makes it purr.

He also once begged me not to tell a soul about his tailoring prowess. Apparently it's not super masculine to be known as the guy who sews. He's mended many a jacket and even fashioned Darth Vader capes for my boys one rainy Saturday, but he's kindly asked that this not be my lead-in line at a social gathering. "Have you met Joel? He's really great on the Singer."

Why not be known as the guy who sews? Fussing with needles and thread typically falls into a domestic sphere often stereotypically dominated by women. It's in the same arena with decorating cupcakes, arranging for playdates, buying dance leotards, and grocery shopping. These are the hoops women are said to spin, along with the biological arenas of pregnancy, childbirth, and nursing. And while our culture is blending into more balanced divisions of labor (thank you, Jesus), my husband still prefers "man who plays hockey" over "man who mends." I get it.

"Home" Work

Whether you work in an office or stay/work at home, whether single parenting or married, the reality of "home" work often impacts our ability to keep a balanced rhythm. The fact is inescapable: most mothers administer an extensive checklist of tasks accomplished on behalf of their families.

According to the National Science Foundation (2005) women spend more hours per week on household work (regardless of whether they work full-time or stay at home) than do men. And get this, men actually create an additional seven hours of work per week for women.[1] Now it's not that we don't love our men, but it appears marriage also adds tasks to the list! Another person, another pile of bath towels, another schedule to accommodate. Even in homes with a decidedly even division of labor, research still suggests women will ultimately own a higher percentage of the household tasks. This reality can form another barrier to connection with others if we do not carefully navigate it.

I work out of the home a few days each week and I'm also the grocery shopper, car pool dispatcher, chef (albeit a lousy one), master planner, laundress, and mopper of wooden floors. Thankfully, not the seamstress. My daily list is extensive and often filled with nonnegotiables.

We need to eat.

We are forever out of milk.

We need clean socks.

This is reality for most moms I know.

"Sure, I'd love to meet up at the park or grab coffee, but we're out of bread and the house is a disaster."

What Did I Do before I Had Kids?

Do you remember life before kids? The "run an errand without it taking an hour" era? The days when you could linger at dinner and not have to pay a sitter? At the end of one particularly task-filled day, I flopped into bed and desperately tried to recall what exactly it was that I did with my time before children.

I went to doctor appointments without making seven different phone calls to cover my kids while I got a Z-pack.

I grabbed lunch whenever it struck my fancy.

I slept through the night.

I wore smaller jeans.

Those pre-kid women now seem like inapproachable divas. They shop, sip chai lattes, and get weekly pedicures, maybe even tote around random poodles in handbags. They definitely have time for a million classy friends and no responsibilities. We mostly dig overdue library books out from under the couch. Joel's cousin Robin just got married and moved for a year, sans kids, to Toulouse, France . . . Jealous!

Now Add That Famous "Baby Brain" to This Equation

Louann Brizendine, MD, in her bestselling book *The Female Brain*, reveals how a woman's brain undergoes massive biological changes during pregnancy. Brizendine dishes up fascinating details on our often frantic attempts to manage it all. MRI scans reveal our brains actually decrease in size around six months of pregnancy.[2] "Baby brain" is not just a witty jest, it actually exists!

Isn't that awesome?

During pregnancy the brain also expands what it considers important, explaining how a woman who just nine months earlier was on a career fast track with only a mild interest in kiddos is suddenly and utterly obsessed with her child. A raging hyperprotective Mama Bear seemingly unable to stop uploading newborn pictures to Shutterfly. These brain changes help explain why many women at this stage find their loyalties divided between their babies and the details of their life before kids.

According to Brizendine, "the more you do something, the more cells the brain assigns to the task."[3] So biologically speaking, the more time we spend nurturing and raising our children, the more our brain physically assigns itself to this task.

Mothers today are giving birth later in life and are more educated and professionally equipped than any other generation in US history. From 1968 to 2008 the average age of a first-time mother steadily climbed from around twenty-one years of age to slightly over twenty-five.[4] These stats combined with biology reveal that when a woman becomes a mother her brain *truly* is hijacked. She's expended a considerable chunk of time, energy, and brain cells on pursuits pre-kids (twenty-five years' worth). Then biology earmarks brain cells to the über-important yet tiny world of her newborn. Brizendine says that "in modern society, where women are responsible for not only giving birth to children but working outside the home to support them economically, these changes in the brain create the most profound conflict of a mother's life."[5]

Tricia worked part-time from home when her daughter Anna was ten months old. Her experience sums it up well. "I would spend Anna's waking hours playing with her, feeding her, etc., and the minute she went down for her nap I would try to transition back to career woman. I would literally go from singing 'Itsy-Bitsy Spider' one minute to giving a presentation on a work call the next. In those first few months it felt at times like I was giving myself whiplash trying to race from role to role."

Forgetting Who We Are

In this whiplash of managing our daily tasks, loving our kids, and knowing that our very brains have turned against us, it can feel impossible to remember who we were before children. But take heart, there is a way to thrive by restoring our passions and celebrating our talents.

My dear friend Jana worked for years as a speech therapist with autistic students. She was an expert in her field who decided to step out of that arena once her children were born. Jana devours every learning opportunity like I imagine piranhas might down a hot dog if it fell into the Amazon. She can whip up a curriculum with broken crayons and Polly Pocket's mismatched shoes. Her knowledge of children's books and language development is vast. I always joke that my kids are smarter just for breathing the air in her house.

Jana deeply cherishes her role as a stay-at-home mom. Yet Jana misses her work-self too, having colleagues and the energy that comes with ideas and opportunity. So she struggles to find the balance. The pre-baby Jana did not disappear, she just got relegated to the bottom of the diaper bag with a stray, lint-covered fruit snack. On many days it feels like she all but vanished.

Have you ever felt like you should be allowed to file a Missing Persons Report on yourself? My friend Caryn Dahlstrand Rivadeneira has a brilliant book that touches on this very struggle: *Mama's Got a Fake ID: How to Reveal the Real You Behind All That Mom*[6] (you should totally buy this book—Caryn, you can pay me later). Caryn's passion is to help women recognize that while "Mom" is indeed a tremendously pivotal, life-changing title, this very moniker damages our souls when it becomes all-consuming. Part of forging a healthy rhythm as a mother is remembering that we had an identity before children and that those children will emerge stronger from the nest if we continue to develop that woman throughout motherhood. This is not at the risk of our family but rather to their benefit.

Our children need to see passion and talent played out. They need to watch us develop a skill, pick up a new hobby, exhibit tenacity, intelligence, and strength. If we can model for them the joy in learning and growing throughout all of life, we have a better chance of launching them into adulthood with a bit of gusto and the opportunity to find their own voices. Who you were before you became a mother is tremendously important to who your children will become. The entire trajectory of your life matters to them—as does your ability to cleanly cut the crusts off a PB&J.

I hear Jana wonder if she is still valuable beyond changing a diaper. Was her education wasted? Will she ever use that skill set again? Can her professional pursuits and talent be part of her rhythm as a mom? Many women ask these same questions. How do we tap into our gifts and cling to our dreams during this stage of life without adding more stress or wobbly hoops to our backs?

Seriously. I Don't Have Time for Hobbies.

When the topic of hobbies/gifts/talents/time for pursuing dreams crops up, I have found women wade through one of two conversations: either reconnecting with areas of great giftedness they experienced before children or discovering for the first time that they do have talents and ideas to offer this world. Both are pivotal discussions.

When asked, "So what do you like to do? What are your passions?" I confess that many times I just stare blankly. This is an overwhelming question.

"Napping" is often the first thing that comes to mind. "I am really fired up about taking a nap. And I am quite good at it. Watch me."

But this is a question for which we should all have an accessible answer. For some of us, getting started can mean simply zoning in on what makes our hearts beat faster at the idea of participating. What discussion always grabs your attention? What memories from your past remind you of a time your contribution was celebrated? What academic coursework often came easy to you? What section of books at the library grabs your eye?

Consider keeping a small journal in your diaper bag and for a few months jot down the books, ideas, people, and events that get your mind racing. What are the common threads?

"Pick Up Your Pencils. Begin."

Our culture is not lacking for personality assessment tools. From the Myers-Briggs (http://myersbriggs.org) to Strengths-Finder (http://strengthsfinder.com) to that Gary Smalley thing with the lion, beaver, otter, golden retriever (http://smalley.cc), there are ways to fill in Scantron bubbles and find out where you shine. Many people start out with gift/personality assessments because they offer tangible, concrete statements to jumpstart this journey. Community centers, park districts, churches, and local colleges offer half-day or full-day classes around opportunities like these. Several are offered online as well and many take less than thirty minutes to complete. Consider rallying a group of women to take the same assessment and then process the results together.

If multiple choice and #2 pencils give you bad academic flashbacks, you can always take a more personal approach and ask a *safe*, trusted friend, "What am I good at?" This question feels more than a little self-centered, but the reason for asking is to broaden your reach in this world, so rest in that bit of do-goodedness. Ask this *safe* friend (did I mention this person should be *safe*?) some variation of the following questions:

How do you experience me?
Where do you see me flourishing?

What would you list as my strengths?

Where do you see me struggle?

What do you value most about friendship with me?

This option takes the big-girl pants. It is incredibly unnerving to ask a person for commentary on your life. And what if where she says you struggle is where you thought you were a rockstar? Yet on the flip side, how life-shaping to catch an honest glimpse of your life?

Discover Your "One Big Thing"

I always credit my friend Suanne with this when using her phrase "my one big thing." Suanne has the audacity to suggest we actually focus on one area of passion and release the hounds while setting aside the rest of our ideas for another time. Love it! For Suanne, a ton of energy in one direction is better than frenetic energy scattered around in little bursts—like when you spill cereal on your kitchen floor. Bill Hybels calls this our "holy discontent." He defines it as the place where your greatest passion and the world's greatest needs collide.[7] What is the one area in your life where you can barely contain your energy?

No need to start all grandiose like clean water sources in Zambia or ending poverty. It can simply be the joy you find while reading to your kids which may eventually remind you of those under-resourced kids at school who need reading volunteers. Perhaps you have an hour a week to spare?

Take my friend Jana again. Jana's passion merges with her children's need to learn from their mother, and from there she ends up giving wisdom and ideas to so many moms. Her rhythm helps others. When teaching my oldest to read, I used all the books Jana recommended to me.

She has recently taken this passion to our church and designed resource bags to keep kids engaged during the service. Teaching kids and moms how to learn is Jana's one big thing. Any thoughts on what yours may be?

The Examen

At this point you might be saying, "This is all nice, but how exactly do I zone in on my one big thing?" Here we go. There's a great practice that emerged from Christian monastic communities centuries ago called the Examen (or the examination of consciousness). It's the practice we are already doing via Thumbs Up, Thumbs Down at the conclusion of each chapter. The Examen is asking yourself two basic questions at the end of each day (or at the end of a particular experience). The two questions can sound like one set of these examples:

- For what today am I most grateful? *and* For what today am I least grateful?
- Where did I experience joy today? *and* Where was there sorrow?
- What was the high point of my day? *and* The low point?

I discovered my passion for writing this way. I kid you not, during all my bleary-eyed newborn weeks, the high point of my day was often when I got to check email. Lame. I know it. What I discovered via laptop was that responding to email allowed me to write, even if I was only typing, "Sorry I'll be missing that activity, I just had a baby." I was still writing.

The low point was my consistent struggle to find time for reading a nonparenting book. The irony.

Eventually these emails turned into the very first magazine article I dared to submit, which melded into a whole one-hour class on how to write well, from there a blog and now this book. I kept following the thread. You can do the same. Tug on the strings woven throughout your day. Let your heart follow the pattern. Where is there consistent joy? Over time you will see common themes. This is why it is important, if possible, to journal your Examen responses. Nothing lengthy unless this is your sweet spot.

Own It

I dare you to err on the side of overselling yourself with the ideas in this chapter. How bold and brazen can you be? Have you ever truly owned what you are good at? In our culture women are more likely to downplay their efforts than men. Men typically get that strutting peacock thing going long before the girlfriends do. *Both* ends of the spectrum are wrong and misrepresent our truest selves. Neither are right. One clearly errs on overestimating our importance while the other grossly underestimates it. Both miss the point.

In the Bible, even Jesus addresses this discrepancy. You often find him meeting women and telling them to stand up or rise to their feet while he often suggests that men come down from their places of power. Oh, the subtlety of how we stand. Ponder your own posture for a moment. How do you react when you receive a compliment? What is your stance when learning a new skill?

Take regular moments to rise up into your gifts and passions. To live fully into the rhythm of your life, you need to celebrate all that you are. Rather than experiencing motherhood as a season of "home" work, baby brain, and blurred dreams, we can begin to celebrate all the ways we exercise our gifts and talents. We can live into our true rhythm without adding more hoops to our backs.

FIVE Mom-Tested Tips

1. **Do an Examen today.** Beyond just thumbs up and down on ideas from this book, take a moment tonight (alone or with your family) and simply ask what the best and worst moments of the day were. If it goes well, try it again tomorrow and notice which joys and struggles your family have in common. You might discover an emerging project or passion for your whole family.

2. **Old school photos.** Pull out an old pre-kids photo of yourself doing an activity you loved. Prop that snapshot of you with feathered hair and neon socks up on a shelf, put it in a diaper bag, or find another place you will cross paths with it often. After laughing off the premillennium attire, remember to embrace all that you are beyond just "Mom." Consider the fascination we have with pop-culture icons. Most magazines have offered a bit on guessing those celebs based on their high school yearbook photos. We love this fluff because it tells the wider story of their lives. Do the same for yourself; your kids think you are super famous and fabulous.

3. **30 seconds to Mom.** Dare yourself to engage in a conversation and not even mention your kids. Yes, yes, we love them to bits, but can you meet a stranger and talk it up without asking if that person has a family (which is the undisputed primer for "Hey, I have great kids, let me tell you about

them."). Hold your own, don't lean on your kids to support your story this time. See how long you can go. Way easier typed than done.

4. **Prayer.** Ask God to give you the guts to fully live into who he created you to be. Pray for the bold, sassy attitude it takes to barge right into owning your gifts and talents (we *all* have them) and start claiming your right to living into them. Muster up a little chutzpah and own it. Also pray for humility. Women struggle to find their voices and gifts, so we often undersell ourselves long before becoming egomaniacs. But pray for humility as well. Humble pie is a healthy dessert.

5. **Journal.** Along with your Examen, consider keeping a very specific gratitude list. Each day offers so many experiences for which to be grateful, but try to keep a focused list of the areas where you met with success during the day. Athletic agility with your children, musical accomplishment, helping a friend design her own business cards with your marketing and PR background? Keep a list of where you meet with success. This will help you discover the areas of gifting you naturally gravitate toward.

Thumbs UP Thumbs DOWN

What is one gift/skill I know I've received?

___

___

___

What is one gift/skill I definitely do not have?

___

___

___

BOOKS, PEOPLE, and OTHER RANDOM STUFF

- For a great resource on the Examen, check out *Sleeping with Bread: Holding What Gives You Life* by Dennis Linn, Sheila Fabricant Linn, and Matthew Linn
- StrengthsFinder Resources, http://www.strengthsfinder.com/home.aspx
- Erwin Raphael McManus, *Seizing Your Divine Moment: Dare to Live a Life of Adventure*
- Caryn Dahlstrand Rivadeneira, *Mama's Got a Fake ID: How to Reveal the Real You Behind All That Mom*
- Elisa Morgan, *She Did What She Could: Five Words of Jesus That Will Change Your Life* (or as Elisa likes to call it, "SDWSC")
- Carla Barnhill, *The Myth of the Perfect Mother*

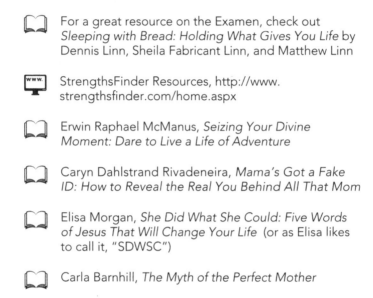

Section Two

Creating a Rhythm for Relationships

5

Game Night

What Is Your Family Famous For?

Family traditions counter alienation and confusion. They help us define who we are; they provide something steady, reliable and safe in a confusing world.

—Susan Lieberman, *New Traditions*

Hey Mama, it's Sunday morning. Where the heck are the donuts? We always have donuts on Sunday morning!

—Danny, age 4

The Flower Hunt Walk

My daughter Lilly and I recently took an evening stroll. It was shortly after daylight savings nudged the sun, and the afternoon finally stretched beyond dinner. Early spring flowers started to flex a little muscle and pack away their winter coats. We called it our "flower hunt walk" and set off to find "all the pretty flowers on the street." Lilly raced from sidewalk to yard, pointing and oohing as daffodils and irises paraded their colors. I marveled at how deftly she moves while strangely still hopping along like a toddler. I cringed as she stomped on a few burgeoning tulips.

After the initial excitement of finding flora, we clasped hands and settled into a pace, walking the block, discussing whether or not the "nice doggie" on the corner would be barking at her. It was an idyllic, triumphant mama moment. Warmer weather, sun setting, my daughter and I walking hand in hand gazing at flowers. It was also nearing 7:00 p.m., and sadly this was the first moment all day that I had slowed my pace long enough to truly engage my child. She'd been up since 7:00 a.m., but the day had been a blur of spilled cereal, errands, school for her brothers, a work event for me, mac'n'cheese. Finally, twelve hours and one sunset later, I lavished undivided attention upon her.

I stared down at her sparkly pink heart sneakers, mismatched pants, and crooked fishy sunglasses. Her fingers, donning chipped silver nail polish, felt so grubby and gloppy from a day of art projects. I remember taking a deep breath and thinking that I wanted to be known for moments like this. I wanted to be the kind of mom who drew long pauses out of life and went on lots of "flower hunt walks." I wanted forever to feel her whole sticky hand wrapped tightly around my pointer finger. I wanted to hear her say, "Hey Mommy, you are pretty like the flowers." (I kid you not, she said this, completely unprompted.)

I want to be the mom who drenches her children with time rather than hurry. The mom whose presence signals rest and peace rather than activity and chores. This is how I want my whole family to be known—a people of rest and grace.

Creating vs. Filtering Culture

Every family has a certain aura or ethos; whether intentional or accidental, they exude a particular feeling that others experience when encountering its members. Every family inevitably creates its own culture.

One family prizes musical accomplishment and drips with talent. A piano is the focal point of this home. Both parents are accomplished musicians and the children are known for their skills. This is the home you come to for lessons or to discuss if that new album is worth downloading.

Other families are bursting with four or five, six or seven kids. Their homes are loving and loud. Supersize deluxe boxes of food from gigantic warehouse stores vanish before groceries are unpacked. Sports equipment heaves open the closet doors of shared bedrooms. The culture of these families includes abundant togetherness, everyone has jobs and tasks, older kids help with younger siblings. There is a unique ethos in each of these families.

I once heard author Andy Crouch speak about shaping culture in general. He believes that every person is a creator of culture. They have unique ways through which they engage and contribute to the world. Crouch wisely suggests that life is less about consuming and more about creating.[1] We have stories to tell; histories to capture; art, music, and athletics to enjoy. This idea transfers to our families as well. Each one makes a unique contribution.

As parents we often believe our task is to filter culture, to determine the good, the bad, or the appropriate for our children to ingest. The very word is a moniker we often find suspect; we raise our eyebrows at certain movies, books, and celebrities. "Is that video game safe for my son to play?" "Does the media make my daughter self-conscious about her weight?"

But what about the fact that we are also called to be contributors to culture? That our families are epicenters of creativity and expression if we unleash and enliven them? My friend Nancy is a strong, creative, gifted woman, one of the best party hosts I know. She constantly looks ahead and wisely counts the short years her four children will be with them at home. Nancy plans everything from holidays to vacations with the grace and sense of purpose it takes to create a culture her kids can cherish forever. Nancy's desire is that her children know what it means to be a family member.

Crafting Your Own Definition

Like discovering your gifts or connecting in the daily schedule, championing your family's culture does not require five hours of extra work per week or upping your caffeine from a grande to a venti. One simple way to get started is by keeping the long-term desires for your family in mind.

Our lives often involve phenomenally shortsighted thinking—dashing from task to task, often leaving one project half-finished because another shiny and more glittery thought snatches our attention. We can lose track of the proverbial bigger picture.

Laundry, seemingly benign, can even hijack the vision of my day. Sure, I may start out with noble intentions . . . clean underwear for all! But laundry piles are stealthy. I move a clean pile of socks to my daughter's room and suddenly I am pairing stray bobby socks . . . with all my free time. This forces me to recognize that I still have ten-plus pair of newborn socks that now only fit her thumb.

Then that shiny, sparkly thing happens, and I yank open the closet looking for other 0–3M items that no longer fit. Thirty minutes later I have a pile for Goodwill in the hallway and am pulling outgrown pajamas and toys from my sons' room. By lunch I am loading up the car for a charity drop off. Meanwhile wet laundry sits in the machine soaking up that mildewy smell. My inbox is flooded with work email, the kids are bored, and we end up ordering carryout. I moan that "nothing got done today."

This shortsighted, task-focused spaziness can swallow entire calendar squares. So, when I have the glorious moment of clarity and vision that a flower hunt walk can bring, I grasp it. I do that shiny, sparkly thing again, only this time with my heart. I focus anew on what I want the very core of my family life to be about. Clean closets do have value, but task obsession will not shape the soul of my child the way stopping to poke at daffodils will.

What are the macro-level themes that inform your family's life? Are you willing to forgo opportunities and even clean closets when they interfere? My friend Jen's long-term view informed her decision to pass up high-profile opportunities so that she could craft her family's culture. Jen said, "My life was really not slowing down, so I needed to spend my time very wisely and carefully with those who nurture my soul and vice versa." Other families skip traveling sports or deem Sundays sacred so that their long-term ideals of resting together are achieved over time.

Rather than hop from activity to activity in our home, my husband consistently asks, "What will the impact of this decision be come bedtime?" When hockey and T-ball overlap, he refuses to let our kids do back-to-back practices. He abhors the hurry and stress that come from leaving early, arriving late, changing gear in the car, "come on let's go!" The value he pushes in our family is to live without unnecessary stress. Skipping one small practice helps us live into the bigger picture—a low-stress family culture.

Getting Started Is Simple

I caught up with Jennifer Grant, author of *Love You More: The Divine Surprise of Adopting My Daughter*. Jennifer is brilliant when it comes to family culture. She offered a few easy yet poignant starter questions for us:

- What are our gifts?
- What makes us laugh?
- In what ways can we all grow and be more fully the people we were created to be?
- How can we better connect to each other and learn how to connect in a healthy way with others?
- How is each one of us distinctly suited to make the world a better place?[2]

We already have many norms in place. What rules do you already live by? No shoes in the house, no TV when friends are over, no snacks after 7:00, Taco Tuesdays.

Choose a few words that you believe currently define your family's culture. Humorous, artistic, loving, entertaining, athletic, helpful, giving, homebodies, world travelers, globally active, good neighbors, slow, fast, outdoorsy, city folks. You get the picture. Now add to that list the missing elements you deeply desire. Define how you want to be known. What long-term goals will make it happen?

Celebrate What You Have Already Created

Another good step is to realize that you *already* have a family culture. Like Saturday morning pancakes or football games at Grandpa John's. Identify what works and protect it fiercely. We are crafting a slower pace at our house, so I've identified several activities we need to yank back. Don't mess with pancakes on Saturday and Chicago Bears games with Grandpa on Sunday.

Another helpful step on the journey of creating a family culture is to be honest with yourself. Brutally honest. While I envision quiet, peace-filled moments with my children, I have to recognize that I've been wired with a tremendous amount of energy (as in, I'm a complete spaz), so "quiet" in our home is going to sound a bit different than quiet does for mothers who are naturally more contemplative and reflective.

We've all had those forced Clark W. Griswold Family Vacation moments. Like when Chevy Chase dragged his family for miles into the woods to fulfill his dream of chopping down the perfect Christmas tree. Knee-deep in snow, with blue lips and chattering teeth, his frigid family trudged along while Clark waxed eloquent about his dream. "We're kicking off our fun, old-fashioned family Christmas by heading out into the country in the old front-wheel drive sleigh to embrace the frosty majesty of the winter landscape and select that most important of Christmas symbols."

Poor Clark, no one cared but him.

Our families are comprised of individuals who, at eight months old, will mostly do what we say because we can carry them along. But when they outgrow the 500-pound infant car seat with carrier, they will walk away if they do not have any say. As our children age, we invite them to join the conversation. If you decide that rest and quiet is a high value and they long for bustling opportunities to get out, explore, be active, and entertain, you will have to establish common ground. No use dragging them through the snow for a Christmas tree if all they remember is that they had no say.

Rule for Life

Another helpful resource for shaping family culture is a practice called the "Rule for Life." Or, as my old friend Vickie called it, "Rule for Always." Adele Calhoun, author of the *Spiritual Disciplines Handbook*, reminds us that we already have many rules we live by.

"Try hard."

"Do your best."

"Be nice."

"Just do it."

Calhoun says that "developing a 'rule for life' is a way of being intentional about the personal rhythms and guidelines that shape our days."[3] She believes these rules are a way of keeping our lives ordered to avoid unintended chaos. Not the sort of chaos that comes from spilled milk or a missing blankie, but the chaos that hangs an anxious haze over our days, the chaos that loiters deep in our hearts.

Rules for life also remind us of our limits and of what the writer of Ecclesiastes says—"There is a time for everything, and a season for every activity under the heavens" (3:1)—thereby ultimately giving us freedom. To let go of all that is beyond our grasp allows us to sink deeply into all that is immediately with us.

Pete Scazzero, an author and pastor from Queens, New York, defines a Rule for Life as a framework that that allows us to grow. For Scazzero, rules offer a trellis, a structure that gives us the strength necessary to grow upward and thrive.[4] Rules also change over time depending on the season, ages of your children, state of your marriage, work hours, and so forth. My friend Rhonda lives by a fabulous rule at her house (that she copied from our friend Lisa's house): "Remember who you are and who you represent."

Here are some other sample rules:

Be fully present to others.

Love God. Love others.

Eat healthy. Live healthy.

Celebrate laughter.

Help others in need whenever you can.

Encourage friends and family.

Pray often.

Love extravagantly.

Of course I also have some unwritten rules I happen to live by, such as "caffeine makes me happy" and "no one poops in the bathtub."

You get the picture. Rules provide the course markers necessary to chase wholeheartedly after what matters and let what hinders you slip away. Just like eating all your dinner frees you for any flavor Popsicle you want. Stick to the rule and a whole world of opportunities awaits.

FIVE Mom-Tested Tips

1. **List your favorites.** Take a few moments to list your favorite family traditions, whether holidays or parts of your everyday routine. What moments do you cherish and why? Notice where you find yourself saying, "I hope my children still do this when they leave home." Make a short list of these moments and look for common themes to emerge. This will tell you a bit about the rules you already cherish as a family.

2. **Inside jokes.** Julie Ann Barnhill spoke at a MOPS General Convention about the nearly two decades of shared giggles and inside stories with her son Ricki. She went on to explain how important it is for a family to have little quips and sayings only they understand. This builds camaraderie and culture. Make a joke. Create a secret handshake, hug, or wink. Insert recurring opportunities to repeat them throughout your week. Like the super-special high five at the preschool drop-off or the crooked smile/wink combo when your child is nervous at practice. These routines become rules in many ways—like when you are stressed, the wink reminds you that you are loved.

3. **Stuck on a feeling.** We have all visited homes that make us feel welcome, homes that have a sense of rhythm and a life-giving culture. When you visit a family who feels open and honest and who seem to live sanely, take note. What are their

routines, how do they manage a day? It's not all perfect there either, but notice what differences you sense and consider how a few new routines might help your home too.

4. **Prayer.** There is a method of prayer called "breath prayer" that is very short and rhythmic. It simply requires you to breathe in by reciting one part of a prayer and breathe out by completing the sentence. For a while my prayer was this: (breathe in) *Gracious God, give me strength;* (breathe out) *and help me bring peace to others.* Clearly nothing fancy. Try to capture one of your hopes or desires in a prayer and literally breathe it in and out for a day, a week, a month.

5. **Journal.** Keep a quote book handy for all the witty, unpredictable things your children say each day/week/month. Make a plan to write down the one-liner as well as the setting if it helps tell the story. Then reread this journal with your children at the end of a year. It brings back memories, opens opportunity for tradition, helps you celebrate the sense of humor or poignant moments unique to your family. I've never met a family who regretted keeping a quote book but have met many who wished they had. This one is a time-tested keeper.

Thumbs UP Thumbs DOWN

What is your most celebrated family tradition or routine?

What is one part of your family routine that you wish you could discontinue or adjust?

BOOKS, PEOPLE, and OTHER RANDOM STUFF

- Pick up *My Quotable Kid: A Parents' Journal of Unforgettable Quotes* by Chronicle Books
- Jennifer Grant, *Love You More: The Divine Surprise of Adopting My Daughter*, as well as her other work on family culture at http://www.jennifergrant.com/
- Andy Crouch, *Culture Making: Recovering Our Creative Calling*
- Lorilee Craker, *Money Secrets of the Amish: Finding True Abundance in Simplicity, Sharing, and Saving*
- Ruth Haley Barton, *Sacred Rhythms: Arranging Our Lives for Spiritual Transformation*

6

Pinocchle and Bingo

Aunts, Uncles, and Extended Family

Boy meets girl. Boy marries girl. Boy and girl angst over which family they visit at Thanksgiving and which one in December and whether or not it's best to serve turkey or goose for the family feast. When first faced with the reality that the family you married into does things differently, the warmth of tradition can take on a chill.

—Marge Kennedy, author

Take care of widows who are destitute. If a widow has family members to take care of her, let them learn that religion begins at their own doorstep and that they should pay back with gratitude some of what they have received. This pleases God immensely.

—1 Timothy 5:3–4 Message

Sharing Toothpaste

Humorist Erma Bombeck once said, "The family. We were a strange little band of characters trudging through life sharing diseases and toothpaste, coveting one another's desserts, hiding shampoo, borrowing money, locking each other out of our rooms, inflicting pain and kissing to heal it in the same instant, loving, laughing, defending, and trying to figure out the common thread that bound us all together."[1]

Sharing toothpaste with anyone but my immediate family freaks me out. The germs. Another family's germs. From a bathroom in a faraway place. I'd rather use the slobbery toothbrush of my toddler than squirt a dab of fresh mint from a nonrelative. I am sure their bacteria is very dangerous. If the tip of their toothpaste tube touched their toothbrush, and now mine, then what? Pandemic!

Extended family are the people we don't share toothpaste with—whether grandparents, cousins, or first cousins once removed. They typically do not share an address or see us in pajamas. They conjure up all sorts of emotional goodies. We may harbor decade-long grudges against them or simply feign contentment to sidestep an argument. (Probably bad form to pick a fight with Grandma.) Or we may love them fearlessly.

We can make dramatic decisions around our proximity to this next layer of loved ones, passing up the swanky loft and hip job for a move back home "to be near the grandparents." Extended families grace our lives in a myriad of ways.

All the Ways We Are Family

Today many mothers find themselves finessing the boundaries of child custody and other fine nuances of divorce/separation. Single parenting, former in-laws, or stepparenting and blending families into a new rhythm brings about joy and challenges as well. Like my friends Nia and Rob, who deftly blend together four young children by navigating in-laws, custody conversations, traditions, and the like.

At times, extended family is at best a struggle. They link us to pain or injustices from the past. One thousand miles away still brushes too closely past some memories. Even in the best situations old stories still linger. Mario Puzo, of *Godfather* fame, once remarked that "every family has bad memories."

Bestselling author Judith Viorst noted that "figuring out our relationships, as a couple, with parents and our in-laws can be challenging even when there's goodwill on all sides. But plenty of couples must figure out these relationships under considerably less than idyllic conditions."[2]

For many of us, our deepest, truest friends also serve as extended family. Sure, genetically we are utterly disconnected, but our children instinctively call them aunties and uncles. These folks know and love your children fiercely. Theirs are the homes where your children have ripped open the door, kicked off shoes, and are wading through the toys while you are still outside slamming car doors. Good friends often fill these extended roles.

The catch with our extendeds is that often there are so very many of them, each with a unique set of quirks and expectations that need to be jostled, ignored, or accommodated.

"Shhh, I know it looks gross."

"Just eat Aunt Ginny's creamy bean casserole and I will sneak you a fruit snack."

"What do you mean you won't be in town for Thanksgiving this year?!"

These always-dynamic family systems require perhaps more balance than we offer those with whom we actually share toothpaste. They help you live in balance yet can push you off kilter. Finesse is required with this ring of beloved connections.

But We Always . . .

Our natural inclination is to fall into the routines (whether good or bad) we were raised with. When Joel and I hung our "First Christmas Together" ornament on the tree, we also had a double-stacked set of holiday plans to navigate.

We both had treasured Christmas Eve traditions with our extended families, held in two separate states (albeit bordering ones). So what's the plan? Try to do both, of course.

Seven years and three kids later, we were still driving about like raving lunatics. The blessing of abundant, accessible family became four separate parties, church, endless food—oh my, that corn-flake potato casserole—and squashed packages blocking the rear window of our station wagon, all wedged with a holiday shoe horn into thirty-six hours. Santa even had to come early to accommodate it all.

"It's because the reindeer get tired so he kicks off the Midwest on the twenty-third." (Just in case you meet our kids and they ask.)

My own mother finally asked why I keep this up. Secretly I suspect she wanted out of hosting. "Why don't you start your own traditions, honey?" I paused, realizing that while I earnestly worked to relive my childhood, loads of sugar and hours in the car had become holiday lore for my children.

Center your traditions on your immediate family and pepper the fringes with your extendeds.

The "B" Word

Do you have boundaries that help protect your traditions and daily routine?

"Sure, stop by randomly if you want, but we may not be home."

"Well, my kids go to bed at 7:00, so dinner with Aunt Sally at 6:30 won't work for us."

"That birthday party sounds smashing, but it's a long day for our toddler."

Psychologists and authors Henry Cloud and John Townsend note that, "we change our behavior when the pain of staying the same becomes greater than the pain of changing. Consequences give us the pain that motivates us to change."[3] Do your current rhythms and routines cause your family some level of pain? Even when coming from a place of familial love and connection? If so, then lovingly, generously, graciously set boundaries so you can maintain your own rhythm. You can haphazardly lament the stress of not setting boundaries for a decade or dare to switch it up and succumb to that deep, true longing for your own traditions.

You are not alone if you have yet to receive the gift of guilt-free family engagements. Guilt comes fast and thick. As a parent in your own right, you find yourself a child again, eager to please. What you are ultimately seeking may be acknowledgment that you are indeed a separate person from your family. A separate family unit. You have the ability, freedom, and integrity to make your own graceful choices about the rhythm you want to live. You, as the mother, actually do know best.

Drawing these boundaries is excruciating. We chicken out. Try again. And then back off once more. A boundary marks off territory. Simply put, it reveals the point at which this is mine and that is yours. Where is your line? Will it be recognized? Healthy boundaries that are respected will remain the nonthreatening reminder they were meant to be. Of course we all know that boundaries can be misunderstood, perceived as offensive or divisive, but forge ahead. Do you want your family to remember you by the way you honored their needs or by the fact that you tried to keep everyone else happy?

Keep at it by picking one event or connecting point at a time.

Choose wisely.

Tread super lightly.

Please tread lightly!

Boundaries offer your immediate family the space you need to work out life while modeling for your own children healthy separation and adult relationships. I watched my dad constantly draw the line with his mother—a wonderful woman but one who could throw down the guilt for not sitting in the "front room" with her every Sunday. "No, Mom," my dad kept saying, holding his line in place.

I *highly* respect both my in-laws and parents for the space they provide to craft our own routine. Pasta is dished up almost every Sunday at my in-laws, without a side dish of guilt. My mom wishes we would stop by more, but life is hectic, so she comes to us. Establishing the proper boundaries helps you cherish rather than lament the rich gifts of extended family.

Lawn Chairs in the Living Room

This hoop of relatives—of cousins, aunts, uncles, grandparents—often brings us the rich heritage and stories that help identify our families.

How did we end up in Cleveland? Austin? San Diego?

When did Great-Grandpa come through Ellis Island?

What was Uncle Erwin like before WWII?

What were our relatives' passionate about?

What did our family stand for?

What did they celebrate or believe in?

My grandmother was one of nine. She and her siblings would run alongside slow-moving locomotives as they came through town, hollering for the crew to toss them chunks of coal that they would use to heat their home during the Depression. A lesson in earnest living. Grandfathers learn rich wisdom on a battlefield. Sisters offer ideas on wading through loss and loneliness. Uncles teach lessons on humor in hardship.

What are the stories and lessons you want to keep? What are the best qualities of your extended family? How does the rhythm they lived with help inform your own routine?

I chatted with Jen, a mom of three, via Facebook for a bit about the trappings of our consumer-oriented lives—namely, our desires for nicely furnished homes and our hesitation to invite people over without a proper sofa. Our chat was just a month after her own beloved father passed away. This is what she wrote:

> I was going through some old photos, a time of reflection and reconnection with my past and looking for Dad in them. I stumbled across a Christmas photo with a *big* tree in the family living room, a house under construction and really poorly decorated. There were other photos in the bunch that had extended family members in them and in one picture I found my Dad, reclined in a LAWN CHAIR with my little sister laying on his belly! I thought to myself, really? Put that lawn chair away, you have company over for Christmas! Then, I remembered what my Dad was so truly all about. Humility, real, genuine, and unpretentious. It was more important that he had his family over, and likely that they got the better chairs.
>
> I have to wonder where my pride came from. I am embarrassed and ashamed that I have not learned more from my Dad. I've never been big on journaling, but intend to start one, called *Lessons I've Learned From Dad.*

Lawn chairs and an unpretentious Christmas. The ethos of these stories are the bookends of family life, the giant volumes that prop up stacks of other stories. We are better because of lawn chairs in the living room. Like Jen, we must find our own way to preserve the rich stories that frame our family photographs.

When They Skip a Beat

For many of us, the network we call family includes a few generations farther up the ladder. The "we managed to survive without cell phones and texting, why can't you?" generation. And beyond them, our network extends perhaps yet another rung. Each generation beyond me I consider a buffer. In my warped little mind, I am still young and somehow not really aging if my mother and grandmother are still around. Two buffers between me and heaven. I'm good for a while.

Then one afternoon your grandmother greets you with a longer pause than usual. Has she really forgotten your name? Words like "dementia" and "Alzheimer's" swarm the dinner table. Or your once-agile parents seem to nap a bit more these days, forget a few more details than seems typical. Someone mentioned a knee replacement last week.

I watched my mom (as I now watch my mother-in-law) care for her own mother. When aging or illness settles in, when cancer or hip surgery takes over the body of your beloved, will you be able to fit that into your rhythm? It's not always just kids that we drive around, bathe, clothe, and tuck into bed.

How does careening toward the unavoidable reality of our own finitude shape each day? I watched my mom give up an entire floor of our home during the busiest season of her life so that my grandmother could move in after breaking her hip.

As your life marches with determination toward the next decade, as the shoreline between you and life's end erodes, will you be ready to give space to care for those who cared for you? Visiting their home? Just sitting with them? Making weekly laundry trips or junk food runs to help them out? You pick it (or maybe, honestly, you don't get to pick it). But you do get to decide whether or not to incorporate loving up to the end into your rhythm.

A friend with a harried connection to her aging parents once said to me, "I just want to be okay with it when they go." In all the messiness of their shared lives, she still recognized the importance of making time, of her own children hearing their stories, of extending grace so that in the twilight of their days she can say goodbye having loved well. She widened her margins, adjusted a few boundaries while keeping others firm, and made room to do life together again.

A Sabbath Together

Boston College sociology professor Juliet Schor lives on the front edge of research about our consumer-inspired lives. In *The Overworked American* Schor's research revealed that for decades (as logic would have it) the industrial and technological advances of a nation resulted directly in more leisure time. Consider for a moment what your great-grandmother had to do to wash her skivvies. Whatever would she do with all that extra time once 1910 rolled around and the first commercial washing machine, awesomely named The Thor, came out? More time for leisure!

Industrial advances typically translate into more time to celebrate, sit around the table, enjoy friendships. For nearly a century productivity and leisure were both on the rise. Then, according to Schor, in the late 1940s there was a dramatic shift in the US. We decided to buck that hundred-year-old trend. While the rest of the developed world focused on more leisure, we made a conscious decision as a nation to begin working more.

Schor states that every time productivity increases we have a choice: to keep output levels the same and work less or to work the same amount of time and produce more. By 1948 productivity solidified its spot on the American altar next to

Coca-Cola and Corvettes. By the 1990s American manufacturing employees were working 320 more hours per year than their European counterparts.[4]

How are we supposed to protect the rhythm we are discovering when our cultural idols are productivity and success? How does a culture fueled by residue from the Protestant work ethic and *Jerseylicious* catch its collective breath and enjoy a Sunday meal with extended family?

Consider taking a weekly Sabbath to focus on these relationships. Sabbath is a vast discipline with many complex angles. It comes to us from the Jewish tradition and ultimately from the Ten Commandments. It simply means to rest, to take a break. To focus on that which brings you joy. To spend time in leisure with those whom you love. Jewish observance of the Sabbath begins on Friday evening at sundown and extends to Saturday evening. During this time the idea is for intense work and striving to cease so celebration and rest can take over.

Consider starting with a day each week where you focus on putting your feet up with extended family members. Order pizza if you don't care much for the kitchen. Go to a movie together. The point is to make a regular, focused point of dwelling well together. Pick whichever day of the week you'd like and make it sacred for your wider family.

In the blur of boundaries, aging, and navigating family dynamics, you will find great life and hope in the idea of making time to stop and treasure the stories and delicious memories of life together.

FIVE Mom-Tested Tips

1. **Heritage field trip.** Consider a family outing to a significant location from your family's past. The home your grandfather built. Your great-uncle's farm. The home you grew up in. The church where your parents were married or your former elementary school. Perhaps even an event as grandiose as checking the registry at Ellis Island to trace your ancestors, or a visit to an ancestry-tracing website. If your current location allows for it, take your children to visit, in person, part of the story that has shaped their lives. Help your children take a few snapshots and archive the event.

2. **Family dinner questions.** Take a stack of note cards or even scraps of paper and write questions that your immediate or extended family can answer when they stop by for dinner. Everything from favorite colors or cartoons to questions about favorite memories. A simple question like "What's your favorite toy?" can suddenly spark conversations—Yo-Yo's vs. LEGOs and stories of playtime from the 1940s or 1950s. Keep these questions in a bowl or box near your kitchen and pull them out when a number of people are gathered at your table.

3. **Get those pictures out of your camera!** Seriously. Don't skip this part. Do it! We all know it, but do we download, upload, and print? Our generation of parents has more memory-capturing

devices at our disposal than any other, yet most moms I know lament that Christmas photos from two years ago are still in the camera. One lost phone, camera, or laptop crash and an entire era of family history disappears. It is absolutely essential for you to archive life if your story is to settle into memory. Commit to taking at least one hour per month to organize and archive. Grab a few other moms to join you and consider extending an opportunity to connect while you click and crop.

4. **Pray.** Take the time to keep a prayer list for the extended family you cherish. Often there are many of these folks, so praying for each of them by name, each night, might keep you up until the wee hours. Consider keeping a list and each night praying for one of the people on that list. Another option is to keep all the Christmas cards you receive over the holidays in a prayer box. Pull a card from the box each night at dinner or bedtime. Often that card might be a photo greeting card from an aunt, cousin, or cherished friends. Pray for the person/family whose card you pull, then start again at the beginning until next Christmas.

5. **Journal.** Find the time to jot down your own favorite memories of your parents, friends, cousins. Our children enter in and out of phases where family dynamics and connections are incredibly intriguing to them. "Why do you call Nana 'Mom'?" "So, is Grandpa your dad then?" They want to know how we are connected to the people

they love. Consider taking one family member a week. Jot down five minutes' worth of stories about that one person at the end of each day. By the end of the week, you will have thirty-plus minutes of stories collected about a loved one to pass along to your children as you all age together.

Thumbs UP Thumbs DOWN

Why is extended family life-giving for me? What do I cherish most about this group of people?

Why is extended family exhausting to me? Where do I struggle with this group?

BOOKS, PEOPLE, and OTHER RANDOM STUFF

- Bobbi Conner, *Unplugged Play: No Batteries. No Plugs. Pure Fun.*
- Leeana Tankersley, *Found Art: Discovering Beauty in Foreign Places*—a masterful example of how the snippets of our lives are absorbed into a divine story. "Found art emerges, a literary collage created from salvaged stories of loss, hope, and belief." (from the back cover)
- Margaret McMillan Persky, *Living in God's Time: A Parent's Guide to Nurturing Children Throughout the Christian Year*
- The Center for a New American Dream, www.newdream.org/

Bret Nicholaus's resources for creating traditions and celebrating family life. Check out two books by him:

- *Who We Are: Questions to Celebrate Your Family* (coauthored with Paul Lowrie)—a book that offers space for your family members to write the story of your family
- *Kidchat: 222 Questions to Spark Creative Conversation*

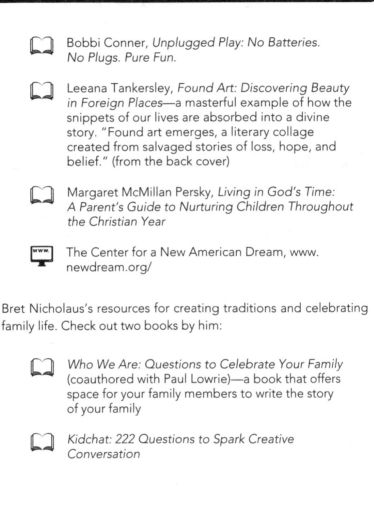

7

Ring Toss

Balancing Our Marriages

I'd trade my husband for a housekeeper.

—Trisha Ashworth and Amy Nobile[1]

Newlyweds become oldyweds, and oldyweds are the reasons that families work.

—Source unknown

The Marriage Caveat

Stating the obvious: Not everyone is married. As of 2006 there were 12.9 million single-parent households in the US (10.4 million are single mothers).[2] My friend Sarah has a three-year-old son but has never been married. She's a rockstar when it comes to mothering but does it all without the consistent daily presence of a spouse.

I sat next to Sarah at a MOPS meeting where the speaker (a dad) shared a vignette about his wife losing it whenever he was late coming home from work. Anything after 5:01 p.m. proved disastrous. A mother of two toddlers and one newborn who, after an afternoon of erratic nap patterns and cutting grapes into fours, longed for reinforcements.

Dad rattled on with hilarious snippets of spousal life as we giggled and rolled. The sort of laughter that swells up when someone explains your predicament so precisely you'd swear they lived in your cabinet. With my hand cupped over my mouth muffling a laugh, I looked over at Sarah to find a big ole tear sliding down her cheek. She too cupped her hand over her mouth. Same gesture. Totally different emotion.

"Five o'clock never comes at my house," said Sarah. "There are no reinforcements. It's never, ever five o'clock."

For some of us five o'clock never comes (so I completely understand if you need to skip right on ahead to chapter 8). And for others of us, five o'clock eventually comes, but our marriages can be in such a state of distress that five o'clock just ups the ante. Stress levels skyrocket, arguments erupt. Our wedding rings are the tiniest of hoops, yet can throw off-kilter any rhythm we've managed to create when we struggle with a spouse. If you are married, keeping a healthy marital rhythm with your spouse is essential to finding balance in your home.

Joel and I see parenting as "us against them," and we try to play on the same team. There are three little people working to hijack us by smashing crackers into car seats and getting our finest apparel all sticky. Our middle child, Danny, often tries to pit us against one another, perhaps suggesting that Daddy would not get mad at him for walking barefoot to the car in February. Saboteur!

"Daddy would so bust you for that. Daddy and I are on the same team," I whisper to him through gritted teeth while holding his snow boots. It feels good to call for backup. Early on, my husband would joke that we lived man-to-man defense and then, as our pediatrician put it, "switched to zone" once our third child was born. Whatever defense you are playing, you will lose if you are out of sync with the only other teammate you have. Our children also stumble when we are out of whack with our spouse. Energy reserved for them gets diverted into stress and arguments.

A marriage sets the overall tone in the home and provides a tremendous amount of structure. David Code's book *To Raise Happy Kids, Put Your Marriage First* directly addresses this topic. Code says the exhausting landscape of raising emotionally healthy children cannot be traversed unless Mom and Dad are in sync.[3] Children know when parents are at odds. Even at very young ages they can sense the imbalance in their little souls. Psychiatrist Blake Woodside notes that "even subtle fractiousness can lead to anxiety disorders, anorexia, and depression, among other problems."[4]

Since these early years of parenting are often filled with utter physical exhaustion by keeping up with the immediate needs of tiny people, romance vanishes. When you haven't slept in weeks and are still sporting a nursing bra, a date night is comical at best. Most moms of young kids that I know would take a nap over sex almost any day. Working on your partnership takes energy you are likely short on at the moment, but you need the payoff to thrive.

But I Work Soooooo Much Harder Than You!

Does your energy slump in the afternoon? I yawn uncontrollably around 3:00 p.m. every day, it feels like someone hooked me up to a reverse IV and started to just suck out my energy. Truth be told, sometimes we even wake up this way and the day rolls on in utter exhaustion. Toddlers and newborns are all-consuming, leaving us open to pick and jab at our spouses. Recognizing the role that physical and emotional fatigue play in our marriages is one place to begin crafting a better rhythm.

My husband stopped his world once our first son, Charlie, was born. Joel took all the appropriate time off work and coddled us both until he returned to hunting and gathering while I started a new chapter at home. We were both in shock, so we hunkered down together. Neither of us cooked or cleaned for weeks, and it took us both just to change a diaper. Still, we were very much on the same team.

Our second son, Danny, was born over a holiday weekend. Joel took two extra days off work, patted me on the back, and dashed out the door come Tuesday. An office of introverted mechanical engineers was looking pretty good to him. By the time our baby girl, Lilly, arrived she hardly made a dent in the routine (or so it seemed). I came home from the hospital, threw in a load of laundry, and started picking up toys.

Two days after bringing her home, our little operation was humming. I felt like John Stamos at the end of a *Full House* episode, all settled and reconciled. Surveying this scene, Joel caught a glimmer of hope. "So it looks like everything is under control here? Mind if I sneak out to play some hockey tonight?"

"Sure, baby." I smiled sweetly like Ma Ingalls. "You go have yourself some fun, childbirth is hard on you too."

I added "Wife of the Year" to the "Mom of the Year" title I had just pronounced upon myself half an hour earlier. Minutes later he was out the door. One hour later we came unglued.

"I don't want carrots with my dinner," my oldest bellowed from the kitchen.

He delivered this edict with enough fervor to cause the baby to start stirring.

"Why do you always make us eat vegetables!" he bellowed while Lilly started crying.

"You will eat them and I don't care if you like them!" I hollered while Lilly commenced screeching.

"I don't like the new baby. I don't like the old baby [a.k.a. his brother] either."

Suddenly both babies were howling (my youngest two are only sixteen months apart).

"Make them babies stop crying," my oldest son, Charlie, demanded.

Then he asked, "Hey Mama, why are you crying?"

How did we get from serene to frantic in a nanosecond? Trying to coax carrots into one child while managing the tears of two others. For some reason this entire conversation was going down in the hallway just outside the bathroom. I started bawling and slumped onto the wooden floor with all three sobbing children on my lap. My stitches hurt, my head hurt, my chest hurt.

We all just sat there and cried.

Eventually the tears dried up and my boys hopped into bed. No one did eat the carrots. Then poor Joel came home and I unleashed my fury upon him. "Too soon for hockey?" he softly joked. Unable to handle his candor, and never mind the fact that I actually urged him to go, I opened up a can of passive-aggressive crazy wife on him. Hollering about my having to do it *all* and his *never* helping.

In my extremely "rational," hormone-filled opinion, my life was infinitely more complicated than his and nothing he would *ever* do could help (remember, this is the man who sews, the man who does laundry, cleans house, and will even shop for tampons).

Many of us have moments like these. We pride ourselves on strength, yet desperately want more help than we receive. We say to our husbands, "Go for it," while secretly many of us keep lists of who does more, works harder.

Most moms I know have thrown similar words around, regardless of the number of children, if she works at home or out of the home or stays at home to work. I've heard the "I have it tougher than you" conversation consistently replayed. The roots can be deep, the reasons myriad, but fighting fatigue with young kids brings this scene to the forefront quick.

First, we all know how easily anger rises if we are short on sleep. If you nursed, my guess is that at least once you have sat up feeding a child while glaring at a husband deep in his REM sleep. I kicked poor Joel once in a sleepless malaise just to give him a taste of my nocturnal life (don't tell me you haven't thought about it).

And let's be honest, for me to offer a solution by saying "try to get some rest, add a nap to your routine" is a nice idea that rarely happens for most women I know. But what you can do is recognize your anger and work toward avoiding situations that trigger it. I have several friends who refuse to plan anything before 10:00 a.m. (other than school, of course). They know their own personal limits. Other couples keep certain days open or free from activity so they can all rest together and find the space they need to manage fatigue.

Second, let respect inform your life. Some moms struggle with the "I work harder than you" conversation because they receive little affirmation from their partner or family. Motherhood is often a thankless job, and while none of us entered it hoping our kid's first words would be "hey thanks, Mom," it does not hurt to get a pat on the back. Every week I have at least one friend who comments that it would be nice to know her spouse understood the challenges she faces each day.

In some situations these women went from managers, lawyers, teachers, professionals, to maternity leave or life at home in a matter of days. And full-time at home is indeed a full day of work. It's not about Oprah and lattes all day long. Helping your hubby understand what exactly you pull off in a day, what your daily rhythm is like without him, can help the two of you respect and appreciate one another and stay in sync. My friend Nancy once said that it is always good to slip out for a day and let Dad run the show from start to finish. How else will he know?

Fragile Turf

Carolyn Pape Cowan and Phillip Cowan (UC Berkeley) monitored 93 couples over a multiyear period through their "Becoming a Family Project," a longitudinal study that tracked first-time parents from pregnancy through the child's first year of elementary school. Their research indicated that marriages often become fragile around the birth of a first child, and they began to notice that it was not the child per se that caused marital rifts but the struggle to keep a relationship vibrant and hopeful during this early parenting season that was the problem.[5] Unmet desires for fun and togetherness created massive tension.

Did anyone ever tell you to go on as many dates as possible right before your first baby was born? To see movies or grab dinner? As if your impending birth was like a closing submarine hatch and you were gasping for your last breaths of fresh air, and freedom. For me, less than seven days after our movie date with Johnny Depp in *Pirates of the Caribbean: Curse of the Black Pearl*, I asked Joel through tear-filled eyes if he ever thought we would see a movie again. I suppose it does not take a longitudinal study to state the obvious, but the Cowan study is helpful on many levels. First, you are not alone if having children has worked over your marriage a bit. Second, if you approach this reality wisely, your partnership can grow and thrive during this life stage.

When expecting parents entered mentor-like relationships with other couples, they were more likely to stay married. Phil Cowan says, "As a parent, you need a safe place to explore some differences and disagreements that most couples know they need to discuss."[6] Couples who found this had stronger marriages. The wisdom here is simple: don't go it alone. Part of your rhythm as a couple may be finding another duo to share stories and struggles with—another place we recognize that life was not meant to be lived in isolation.

Marriages easily go askew, whether from too much focus on the children, lack of teamwork, pressure from our culture—on it goes. And I'm only offering fifteen-ish pages to a massive conversation where thousands of experts have offered centuries of wisdom. I also recognize that some of your marriages are in deep crisis. My witty little banter about how to find your rhythm may seem irrelevant if you are in the throes of separation, abuse, or neglect. So please, take a moment to consider if you need more robust help than this chapter offers and find the resources that will truly help shape you. No shame in that! Sometimes it takes more than a few ideas in a book to forge ahead.

An Expert Opinion

Here is a commercial break with some excellent resources you can consider to take you further into this conversation.

1. **Henry Cloud and John Townsend**'s resources are easy places to find encouragement and realize you are not alone if you struggle in your marriage! Check out their website: http://cloudtownsend.com. Two solid starting points by them: *Boundaries in Marriage* and *Rescuing Your Love Life: Changing Those Dumb Attitudes and Behaviors That Will Sink Your Marriage*.
2. **Gary Chapman** is another powerful voice for marriages today: http://5lovelanguages.com. His conferences, resources, and books help foster healthy conversations for couples, and his book *The Five Love Languages: The Secret to Love That Lasts* definitely informed our marriage. You can even get started on this conversation by taking a short assessment on Chapman's website (http://www.5lovelanguages.com/assessments/love/).
3. **Dr. John Gottman**'s work on marriage is outstanding. Gottman is nationally recognized as a leader in conversations on parenting and marriage. His work on emotional intelligence as well as his resource *The Seven Principles for Making Marriage Work* have fueled many a healthy marriage. http://gottman.com
4. **Shaunti Feldhahn** also provides an array of resources for both men and women on how they interact and think differently everywhere from the office to the bedroom. http://www.shaunti.com/

"Okay, Okay, But I Am Reading *Your* Book"

"Yes, these other resources are well and good," you say, "but I am reading *your* book, so please tell me something helpful since I actually have this one in my hands and the others require opening my wallet." My particular brand of expertise comes from fifteen years of loving a man who puts bleu cheese on everything, drives a car I hate, and would eat Cheddarwurst (we live close to Wisconsin) all summer long if I let him.

He, to be fair, would lament that I wear the same gray hoodie 200-plus days a year, cannot keep track of receipts, drink way too much coffee, and am forever on the phone. Yet every single morning he tells me he loves me and usually we still like one another come evening. Something is working, so here are five (non-expert) rhythms that work for us:

❶ Celebrate Your Connection: Play Together!

Remember what drew you together in the first place. Joel and I packed it up and moved to Colorado shortly after we married, spending the first few years of our marriage on skis and mountain bikes. Heck, we met when he was a waterski instructor and I an adventure guide at a summer camp. If we don't get to play together, we feel jumbled up, so we try our hardest to reconnect in these same ways.

Yes, easier said than done. Like the time we proved our inept parenting by hauling a three-month-old to Jackson Hole, Wyoming. We met my sister there and took turns holding the baby while the others would ski. Poor baby girl spent two days at the base of a mountain while Mom and Dad caught a few runs. It was a short trip, less than seventy-two hours. Joel and I were exhausted and could barely keep up with the powder we once obsessed over, but I will never forget the utterly giddy middle school smiles we instantly flashed one another after our first run of the day. "I love you, man."

Whether skiing or movies, the symphony, antique collecting, soccer, reading, gardening, or catching the upcoming underground, grungy indie bands like you did in college, you've got to make playing together part of your rhythm as a couple. Remember, you were two people with passions and hobbies before kids, and God willing, you will be that again. Recover your old rhythms wherever you can.

❷ Covet Your Calendar

How are you with the calendar? We have one on our kitchen wall, one on my laptop, one my husband keeps at work, one on my phone (somehow not synched to my laptop), and I have an old-school notebook version in my shoulder bag for work. That would be five calendars. And our turn for snack day still gets missed.

Joel has thrown his type A linear thinking into the process, and every Monday sends out a "Here's the Week" email that we send back and forth until we have every event covered or canceled.

A simple check-in like this may help you stay connected and recognize if the rhythm of your family is off balance—in which case you can wisely cancel events to give you the space to rest (and avoid that anger we spoke about earlier in this chapter).

❸ Ask for Help!

Remember the passive-aggressive, weepy, "go play hockey" wife? Well, she kept at it with the "Sure, you go right ahead" followed by "You never help me" banter. It got old and I had an epiphany with Joel one afternoon. It turns out that he cannot actually read my mind. He does not *always* recognize what needs to be done. So, we have to occasionally string together a bunch of nouns and verbs like "hey, can you please pick up the dry cleaning / put the sheets in the dryer / empty the dishwasher for me."

Joel is a phenomenally capable parent, but our setup is such that he's out in an office all day and I am at home many days. I manage the "wifey" details from 6:30 a.m. to 5:30 p.m. and expect him to come home and know precisely what needs to be done. Super unfair to him. If you struggle in a similar way, then clearly and lovingly define what you need and ease the tension of impossible expectations.

❹ Discover Your Love Language

I must underscore how pivotal this conversation can be for your marriage. Gary Chapman suggests that every person has a primary love language. There are five: physical touch, words of affirmation, acts of service, quality time, receiving gifts. Chapman believes that each of us "speaks" one of these languages, and that in order to understand our spouse, we need to know their primary language.

For example, my primary love language is words of affirmation. I will communicate my love to Joel by cheering him on—"You're the best" or "You are so fabulous." This is my natural expression of love, which also means that I like to receive love this way. When he says, "You are the best wife ever" or "You look great in that dress," I feel loved. This is not to say I cannot receive love in other ways, but my personality will most easily hear "I love you" through words of affirmation.

Joel's gig is acts of service. He expresses love by serving, doing little acts of kindness and help along the way. Two different languages are spoken in our house. A past argument went a little something like this:

Me: Honey, I don't feel like you love me.

Joel: Huh? Sooooo, like where is this coming from? I was just loading the dishwasher.

Me: Mmmm, well, lately I don't feel very connected to you. You never tell me that you think I am great or really say what you love about me [hello, narcissistic tendencies].

Joel: Well, I filled your car up with gas yesterday. Did you even notice? You hate going to the gas station, so before work I snuck your car to the gas station.

Me: Why do I even care about gas? Is fuel romantic?! Aren't I pretty and fabulous? Tell me how fabulous I am!

Joel: Why would I do that when I filled your car up with gas and, oh yeah, I also put air in your bicycle tires. Did you even notice that?

Me: You filled my tires! I could have done that [well, not really]. Tell me I'm pretty! Tell me you love me.

Joel: But I do love you, this is why I filled up your tires and your car.

Once you translate the love languages you speak, it can transform these sorts of daily longings. You can offer love how the other hears it best as well as staying true to your own expressions.

❺ Do Church Together

Joel and I come from dramatically different faith backgrounds. The tiny Italian-American church of his youth is comprised of many first-generation immigrants. Hordes of little old Italian ladies kiss you on each cheek upon arrival.

"Gioia!" they holler. Black high heels clack and echo across the tile floor as they wade through a sea of other kisses to grab your cheeks (your face cheeks, that is). It's *Under the Tuscan Sun* meets *Eat, Pray, Love* meets Jesus. Very warm and intimate in an expat sort of way.

The church I joined as an adolescent was dramatically different than Joel's. A megachurch hopping with activity, programs, and people. No Sicilian welcome committee but a flurry of activity and jelly donuts. No cheek kisses but lots of summer camps and Sunday school options.

It took us almost ten years to validate one another's worship expressions and settle into a pew together. To realize that church was not ultimately about size or shape or how high people lifted up their hands while singing. What mattered was that we got to worship with a community we loved right alongside us.

If you do not currently belong to a church, I urge you to find a faith community and fit it into your rhythm. And if you have a healthy church, go regularly—not because lightning bolts will peal from the sky if you miss, but because healthy churches offer tremendous community and growth opportunities for your marriage and your family. Fruitful marriage and parenting conversations take place in many congregations. Classes and even retreats on what it takes to make a marriage last are often part of vibrant faith communities.

And, more importantly, you will find other couples with whom you can connect (remember that Cowan study/mentor idea). Perhaps even a weekly small group gathering with other couples. And should your marriage find itself in crisis, the friendships, therapists, pastors, and other members of that church might just have the wisdom and encouragement you need to make it work.

So there you have it, five bits of wisdom gleaned from one married journey. Whether an item from this list or one of the resources previously mentioned, I urge you to focus on staying in sync with your spouse. It is one of the most important hoops that you will ever spin, and it puts forth the cadence for so many other areas of life.

FIVE Mom-Tested Tips

You've got 'em up above. Aren't we lucky today?

Thumbs UP   Thumbs DOWN

What is the best memory/moment from your marriage?

When have you felt the least connected to one another?

BOOKS, PEOPLE, and OTHER RANDOM STUFF

- Mike Mason, *Practicing the Presence of People: How We Learn to Love*
- Henry Cloud and John Townsend, *Boundaries in Marriage*
- Gary Chapman, *Things I Wish I'd Known Before We Got Married*

8

Telephone

BFFs and Other Anxious Acronyms

Friends are the family we choose for ourselves.

—Edna Buchanan

Wounds from a friend can be trusted,
but an enemy multiplies kisses.

—Proverbs 27:6

BFFs

I have this paranoid neurotic response to the term "best friend." If I'm chatting with another woman and she mentions her "best friend," I instantly think, "How could she totally ditch me like that, I could have been her BFF!" It's likely I have no intention of becoming this woman's best friend or even friend at all. She is just the instructor for my Step Class or a woman in line at Costco. Perhaps I don't even know her name.

Like in college when your crush walked into European History with his arm around another girl, something strangely competitive and insecure happens when I hear the letters BFF.

Female friendships rank among the most celebrated and meticulous of all human connections. We know the tremendous boost to our souls that a deep friendship will offer and also feel the sickening sting of broken promises and expectations. Dee Brestin wrote a time-honored book about this subject called *The Friendships of Women*. She shares the story of her daughter Sally receiving a note from a classmate, Gwen. It asked Sally to indicate her intentions (a bold move). Was Sally

1. her best friend
2. her good friend
3. sort of a friend
4. not at all a friend

This incident, of course, indicates the developmental stage of an elementary school child but also betrays long questions many women carry for decades beyond grammar school.

"Are we friends?"

"Can I count on you or just sort of count on you?"

"Will you end up talking about me when I leave?"

"Will we have coffee together like Ya-Ya's in our eighties?"

"What if I mark 'best friend' but you mark 'not a friend at all'?"

Unprompted, my daughter Lilly recently yelped from the backseat of our car that her cousin Bella was "her very best friend." The girls sit side by side in a two-year-old tot class, not even *real* preschool, and my daughter already presents this language of friendship acquisition. Bella apparently agreed by informing my sister-in-law Christine that she and Lilly would be wearing matching pajamas on PJ Day. In a Two's Class! Lilly's other "BFF" and a treasured playmate recently reported to Lilly that she was her "second best friend" while my son Danny squeaked in as her "fifth best friend."

So I shake my head on the morning of PJ Day, texting to find out if we will be wearing the long-sleeve monkey pj's or the capped sleeves. Where does this obsession come from? Meanwhile, my friend is also texting, "Hey, what r u wearing 2 Bunco 2nite?"

TTYL—Conversation as Connection

Brace yourself. Here comes the stereotype . . . women talk. Quite a bit. That said, our culture often misinterprets the reason. It is assumed the conversations of women are mostly gossip, erratic and meaningless chatter born out of boredom or an inability to serve up thoughtful wisdom. And while there is such a thing as "idle chatter," most women I know are way too busy to just listen to themselves talk. Even trivial jabber about handbags is usually not about the handbag at all but about meeting the need for a deeper connection. Pulitzer Prize–winning columnist Ellen Goodman says:

> In truth, talk between women is easily trivialized by our culture. There is a drumbeat of disapproval—sometimes mixed with bewilderment or even envy—that surrounds women who spend long minutes, hours, on the phone. It trails after women who sit down together with pizza or coffee, women

> who stand in the ladies' room at work mulling over the details of their daily life. They are chattering, indulging in a gabfest, gossiping, prattling. Their telephone bills are waaay too high.[1]

In truth, women often talk because they have made a conscious or subconscious decision to process life together, out loud. Contrary to the cultural quips, women often find themselves more grounded because of their talk time. Friendships are strengthened. Daily routines infused with energy. It is good for the soul when you chat it up with your girlfriends!

Now flip back to chapter 2 and recall our conversation about feeling alone on that park bench. This motherhood thing will isolate us if we allow it to go down that way. Our culture prizes efficiency and accomplishment. Americans are tremendously task-oriented, chasing after an elusive bottomline. So taking the time to deepen friendships by simply talking, to Goodman's point, seems trivial, superfluous.

What's the immediate measurable output for that?

Can you quantify the net gain of twenty minutes on the phone?

Nose to the grindstone.

Keep at it.

No time to yammer away today!

And even if you had the time, some of you are stuck inside with a newborn. Who would you even be talking to anyway?

I was among the first of my friends to pop out a baby, and the day he was born I lost a ton of conversational connections. My old co-workers or classmates did not want to listen as I moaned about my stitches. My neighbors were still mostly strangers and it felt quite counterproductive, not to mention self-indulgent, to be calling someone at work just to chat it up at 2:00 p.m. on a Monday. I was desperate to connect, so I would strike up a three-minute friendship with the checkout lady at Target. She had to listen to me since I was buying stuff.

Crowded Loneliness

Pastor Randy Frazee says our task-oriented, overworked American lives leave us "steeped in crowded loneliness."[2] Frazee suggests the average person runs in at least thirty-five different relational circles per day. The spouses, teachers, co-workers, bus drivers, babysitters, bank tellers, neighbors, pastors, friends, librarians, crossing guards, carpool members, that checkout lady at Target, and the myriad of other individuals and groups are these circles.

We are so bloated with tasks and to-do lists that we swing in thirty-five relational circles a day, yet hardly connect in any of them. Most of us smile and nod politely to the folks we encounter but rarely take the connection further. This is not all bad—I am not suggesting you sidle up to your daily list of thirty-five people and invite them to dinner. The barista might pretend she did not hear you invite her over for dinner anyway. But we must recognize the irony of a lonely culture living crowded lives. What keeps us from forging any connection at all? Loneliness is often cited as an epidemic in our culture, so how is that possible when we see so many people every day?

One University of California, San Diego research project even suggests that loneliness may be contagious. The facial expressions and body language that betray loneliness could spread feelings of isolation and insecurity throughout a particular social network.[3] If the old adage "laughter is contagious" applies, then I am afraid loneliness is catchy too.

So why not get connected? It's scary to befriend another person. We are biologically and spiritually wired for relationship. The very design of our souls (whether introverted or extroverted) begs for connection, so the more it stings when we are met with rejection. Is it worth the risk?

And that heartache can stick. The backstabbing ache many of us incurred from a few classmates in middle school can inform our current relational efforts. I still hear the jarring metal sound of burnt orange lockers popping open during passing period. Totally remember the jeans I was wearing the first time I hid in the bathroom to eat because mean girls had descended upon my lunch table.

Two-tone Guess jeans.

Cherry-vanilla yogurt, an orange, and a fruit roll-up.

Last stall against the wall.

A long lunch hour.

With moments like this in our mental repertoire who really feels like gunning for new BFFs anyway?

ASAP—Find a Friend, Fast

Eventually many of us take a deep breath, sidestep our fears, and hope to meet an ally. That mom at the park or from gymnastics class seems nice, her kids are cool. Now what? Genuine friendship takes time to cultivate. In our rapid-fire culture that dishes up everything through a drive-thru window, it is hard to develop the patience to let true friendship take root. When I moved from Chicago to Denver, I wanted to press fast forward on my time there. I'd met a circle of women who seemed compatible, yet we still had to swap information: marital status, siblings, career aspirations, favorite books, stories about our own mothers. We needed time to build history together.

Clea Hantman says friendship is a waiting game, "but we want stuff quick and fast—from burgers to friends."[4] She goes on to say, "Know that it's perfectly normal and right-on for friendships to take time."[5] So take the risk to connect and then sit back and give that friendship the space and time it takes to grow. Settle into a rhythm of friendship and wait.

Getting to Know Your Friendship Rhythm

So, how do we find and cultivate healthy friendships in this hectic life stage? Connecting requires a commitment to caring, to extending forgiveness, navigating selfishness, suppressing jealousy. This can feel like another heavy hula hoop. My lifelong, I-could-never-do-life-without-her friend Amy is a dainty size 2 after four children and she always looks tan. She has an old green Jeep Wrangler that I want to drive around in July. Jealousy could easily snatch this relationship. Another dream of a friend, Nancy, has a fantastic old home, restored to perfection, gorgeous furnishings, super warm. I wish I lived there too. You know the routine here. To water the depths of our connections, we must protect them from the dark places in our hearts.

Mom Profiling and Honest Living

Caryn Rivadeneira talks about helping other moms get real by living honestly. She mentions the fact that moms are often judgmental and that gossip about parenting styles, marriages, or discipline methods can deluge our hearts.[6] We might judge another woman by her sweatshirt and her seemingly harsh tone of voice. Never mind that she may have had the stomach flu yesterday, we judge. Emmy Award–winning writer Teresa Strasser wrote a brilliant little piece on "mom profiling." Catching the whole article will make you both laugh and wince (http://tinyurl.com/3qgdvr5). Here is a snippet of how this all goes down:

> [Take, for example, the] incredibly beautiful blond mom at baby music class who smiles at me extra big and for a fraction of a moment longer than the social norm? That lady is lonely. She's an actress who has very few friends because she's so pretty she makes insecure women uncomfortable.

> She will approach me and compliment my son's old-school brown leather boots to break the ice. She will approach me because, perhaps unconsciously, she's taped off the crime scene around me. She knows without knowing why that I'm lonely, too. And I'm approachable, because my diaper bag is tasteful, but has one broken zipper and an obvious Desitin smear.[7]

We can be the worst. Yet we also can toss the life preserver like no other person can in this life stage.

But I'm Not Exactly a Raging Extrovert!

On the flip side of all this talking and connecting is the anxiety that comes with trying to be a woman you were not designed to be. This is not a call to gregarious extroversion but rather an invitation to live within the desires, limits, and longings of your own life. Your best self is your true self.

I recently read a *Washington Post* interview transcript with Rosalind Wiseman, parenting expert and author of numerous resources on navigating friendships and adolescent life (*Queen Bees and Wannabes* is her epic tome). When asked by a mom, "How do I make sure my daughter does not become a victim of my own lack of socialization/shyness?" Wiseman offered a helpful response: "Well, first of all, I think you get to honor who you are, right? Not try to be someone who you're not. You don't have to become the woman who has playgroups at your house all the time. Take it slow. If you're comfortable, invite one parent—since your kids are young, it makes sense to have one parent over for tea or coffee at the same time. And you know, shy parents do not necessarily make bad parents. I think that's important to remember."[8] *Very* important. Be who you are.

So let the rhythm of your life include ample space for grace. Stay true to yourself and make a conscious decision to give people that cliché "benefit of the doubt." This, in turn, also lightens our own load by opening our hearts and releasing the weight of negative thoughts.

A Grace-Filled Mom—Traci Boers

Traci lived across the street for my entire childhood, so she also ambled around with that hot-pink hula hoop of my younger days. From Barbies to playing Kick the Can and sledding, Traci was there. Growing up, you don't realize the tremendous gift of sitting side by side on the patio with a pile of freckly, ponytail neighborhood girls and a freeze pop, waiting for a summer thunderstorm to envelop your backyard. You take for granted the scrawny legs and easy smiles of a pre-teen August afternoon.

I shared nearly two decades of summer days with Traci, and when life normally splits up childhood companions, Traci kept calling. College, marriage, moving, and beyond. She had no intention of letting life bump her off the patio. In many refreshing ways, Tra stayed in the backyard of our youth. Her sister Donna would joke that her only desires were a good pedicure and a chai latte. She laughed more than four-year-old boys do at any story about poop.

Traci's view on life and friendship offers wisdom for us moms. Never, ever in a hurry (seriously, she never rushed), Tra took the time to capture every moment of her day and fill it with purpose. Each day was pregnant with possibility, so why blaze past that? Her friendship came with two life principles you can try: (1) live slowly, and (2) live a grace-filled life. If we focus on just these two concepts (speed and grace), we can bring some balance and rhythm to our friendships—perhaps taking Strasser's blond, new music class friend and journeying with her.

Slow, Grace-Filled Friendships

I recall one summer afternoon when my husband came home from work early. Traci was visiting with her brood, so there were six kids between the two of us. Every riding toy was on the driveway, spilled bubbles and sidewalk chalk too. While the kids ran amuck, Traci and I sat like the *Real Housewives of Someplace Glamorous* on my back deck. It was 90 degrees and we had slumped into my deck chairs after whipping up lunch and mending conflict over the last blue raspberry Popsicle. We sighed and leaned back for all of fifteen minutes until my husband Joel pulled up. Climbing out of his car, he looked over at us and jokingly said, "Oh yes, now I see how hard it really is to stay at home all day with the kids."

My whole body reacted to his comment (meant as *only* a joke). I suddenly felt as though I had to defend my sitting down, explain why Traci had come over, look busy, "Does anyone need more sunblock?" The pressure to accomplish haunts me. Traci? Not so much. She just giggled and with her trademark elongated words said to Joel, "Weeell, you know us, always fun and games." Then she turned back to me and kept on chatting. Did not stand up, flinch, or even speed up her sentences.

Traci never felt guilty for just being. Her laundry got folded and her kids were smart and savvy. Interesting how the same results I was working toward so frantically, Traci found easily. The pressure of our culture did not overtake her, so friendship was always available.

Traci was also gentle. She did not yell, ever. Kids, spouse, the cable guy who was two hours late. It did not matter. I saw her freak out only once after I had our first son. Traci was four months pregnant with her first child. She took one look at me all pale and sallow, sporting that hideous hospital gown, with my greasy hair and a forced smile. She took it all in and winced. "Oh no, neighbor, is it really this bad? It's going to be bad, isn't it?" Like a great friend, I replied, "Yeah, it's pretty bad. You are totally in for it." She panicked for maybe five minutes, then said, "Oh weeell."

Access to a gentle life is not a mystery. It comes via little whispers all day long. A deep breath. A conscious decision not to panic. Closing our eyes for more than a second. Pausing to think and soak in a moment, mining it for what is good and life-giving while releasing the pain and stress. Deciding not to race past or profile the other moms we meet.

Spoiler Alert

Traci soaked up the last drop of every day like that gurgling sound a straw makes in your cup when you suck up the last bubbles of soda. One afternoon Traci was changing her daughter's diaper when her heart unexpectedly gave out, leaving behind three adorable children and her loving husband. It was the most profound loss of my life. I remember lying on our wooden floor, heaving sobs that seemed would never end. I still cannot mop that particular spot without crying.

Traci lived more in thirty-five years than many people ever will. In my heart I imagine her with a giant straw slurping the last drops of a sunset. I know that if asked today, Tra would not do anything different. Her model of friendship is simple and profound. Take your time. Live gently. "Your kids are only little once," she would say. Why rush it? What do you get for all your hurry?

Finding your way through thirty-five relationships a day may simply mean that you slow it down and be fully present to the one who needs your attention. Do not rush friendship. Take your time. Life moves fast enough on its own.

FIVE Mom-Tested Tips

1. **Give her your optimism.** Next time you find yourself frustrated with another mom or tempted to judge/profile her actions, take a moment to consider what the circumstances of her life may be. Is she really a miserable person or just snippy because her child is sick? Was her father just diagnosed with cancer? Consider the backstory you do not see and give her some space. Think positive about her. Perhaps consider offering her help or at least holding the door while she makes a break for it with a screaming toddler. And NEVER underestimate the power of a simple smile.

2. **Take a friend along.** Find one part of your daily routine and make a conscious decision to invite another woman along with you, whether a carpool to work, walk to school, class at the gym, music lesson for your kids. Call another woman and forge some new ground and perhaps even memories together, providing the opportunity to move from one of the thirty-five casual circles to a true friend. This can kick up a few nerves and, of course, fear of rejection. But take the risk to invite another person into your daily routine.

3. **Say goodbye.** Not every connection is healthy. Some need to diminish over time. Others fade into memory because you no longer live near one another or cross paths like you once did. Judith Viorst calls them "necessary losses," an apt term since you have relational limits. Some connections naturally

recede, let them dissipate. It is a natural growing and grieving process, so consider for a moment the amount of time you spend chasing after connections that may best be left to photo albums.

4 **Pray.** Pray for your friends, even if short snippets are all you can manage. "God, help her to heal" or "Help her to be still or happy or strong, help her believe she's a good mom." It takes less than one minute to pray for another mom. What mom could not use a boost? Consider a one-sentence prayer for one of your friends and pray it when you are about to see her. And consider adding yourself to the mix. "God, help me to listen well to her worried heart." Run it through your mind on the way to spending time together and pray for her once you leave.

5 **Journal.** I often describe my friends with lots of descriptive language, even to people who already know them, just like back in the day when people would be named for their family and land. William from Gloucester or David son of Robert. My Little Friend Amy. My Friend Suanne Who Asks Really Good Questions. My Hope-filled Friend Liz. My Determined Friend Nancy. It reminds me of the qualities I love about them and invites me to emulate them in my daily life. Make a list of the adjectives that describe your friends. Think about these phrases for a day and explore the thoughts this stirs up for you. It helps you appreciate the beauty of their lives and honors the good work they do in their own souls. Write out a list of elaborate, honoring titles for them.

Thumbs UP Thumbs DOWN

Which women do you find it most easy to connect with in your daily routine?

____

____

____

Which women offer companionship that you would prefer to avoid?

____

____

____

BOOKS, PEOPLE, and OTHER RANDOM STUFF

Dee Brestin's resources on friendships and women, http://www.deebrestin.com/

Anita Lustrea, *What Women Tell Me: Finding Freedom from the Secrets We Keep* has a great chapter on the generous friendship a woman named Faith offered to her at a hard time. Very inspiring.

Mindy Caliguire, *Spiritual Friendship* via Soul Care Resources, http://www.soulcare.com/

Margot Starbuck, *Unsqueezed: Springing Free from Skinny Jeans, Nose Jobs, Highlights and Stilettos*

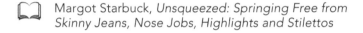

9

Hopscotch

Connecting with Your Community

There are two ways to get enough: one is to continue to accumulate more and more. The other is to desire less.

—G. K. Chesterton

Oh! Teach us to live well! Teach us to live wisely and well!

—Psalm 90:12 Message

Bygone Days

Growing up in Chicago, we quickly learned that while we don't have palm trees or access to the ocean, at least we own some superfamous architecture. Our skyline is dotted with acclaimed pillars and skyscrapers. For twenty-five years the Sears Tower pulled rank as the tallest building in the world. We've got the Smurfit-Stone Building too, that cool diamond-shaped skyscraper that Elisabeth Shue shimmied down in *Adventures in Babysitting* ('80s movie fans, unite). And Frank Lloyd Wright is the poster child of famous suburban architecture, with visitors still swarming his stomping grounds of nearby Oak Park.

We live in a historic-ish home, an old bungalow circa 1929. Our home holds old stories that shimmy up in the form of musty smells from the basement during a rainstorm. Like many old bungalows, our home once boasted a lovely front porch. About ten years before we bought our place, the previous owners walled in the front porch to grab some extra square footage, then attached a deck out back. This is tantamount to a house folding its arms with furrowed brows and saying that it does not want to play outside with you anymore.

There was an era when homeowners up and down my block sat on front stoops and porches. At one point in Chicago history, nearly one-third of the homes in our area were bungalows. If you wanted news, gossip, or just conversation, you plunked yourself out front and chatted it up. This underlying sense of community is increasingly difficult to find. Today if I look out the bay window that the previous owners swapped out for our porch, I cannot see a single bungalow that still has a front porch. They've all been gobbled up for additional space or demolished in favor of a larger new construction.

Cultural Shifts

In its own way architecture reveals what a culture deems important. In the eighty-plus years since our home was built, American culture shifted dramatically. The average home size in the US has more than doubled since the 1950s, now averaging around 2,300 square feet. It was once a given that children shared rooms. Or that a family of five or six would survive with just one bathroom.[1] That families would stay in urban centers, apartment complexes, or row houses rather than dash off to tract housing on abandoned farmland.

Today not so much. As families moved from city centers to the suburbs and beyond, homes grew in size as did our cultural appetite for bigger and better. To keep up, owners of old homes closed in porches and built out dormers. Rural communities have also shifted as high school and college graduates leave rural America in favor of these same suburbs and urban centers. Along the way Americans have found themselves more isolated and deeper in debt than in any other era of US history (hello, recent housing crisis).

The larger the home, the harder a family must work at staying connected. There is a very real temptation, which I completely understand, to give kids abundant space and resources. But it may actually end up isolating families. You need intentional rules to keep connected. My boys share a room even though we could provide each with his own bedroom. It's important to learn how to handle a snoring brother and respect space. We do not allow televisions or computers in their bedrooms. I keep a hearty supply of toys in what would be our dining room. Who needs a formal dining space when you can fill it with art projects and coloring books? This way my kids can doodle just inches away while I fake it in the kitchen. My husband once proudly said, about our home layout, that "I like having all my people close by."

Technology also pulls many of us away from the front steps. Sure, it also broadens our world and via Skype we can chat with a cousin in Argentina, but access to Argentina pulls us indoors. If we want to know how Kate and William's wedding went down, we Google it rather than chat about it on the front porch. Information on my school district comes to me via email or text, and I can see my neighbor's Halloween costumes on Facebook, so why stop over to take pictures. Before TiVo and the DVR, if you missed a news story, you had to call a friend for the scoop. Access to information usually required engagement with another person.

Today we can ascertain a tremendous amount of information about our world without talking to another human being. I'm borderline obsessed with technology, will you friend me on Facebook? So I get how great it is, but the nearly insurmountable drawback is the barrier it can raise to physical connection and conversation with others. From architecture to technology, our culture presents several barriers that us moms must be intentional about navigating well.

Creating a Front Porch Rhythm

"Front porch" really just refers to public space. The foyer of your condo complex, the garden space outside your apartment, your balcony, or in a rural setting perhaps the bus stop or another social place for the homes in your area. I recognize not everyone is a suburbanite with a driveway. But according to the Brookings Institution, 84 percent of Americans do live within the boundaries of metropolitan areas with a population of 50,000 or more.[2] So a huge majority of us have nearby neighbors with whom we might just sit on the front porch if we had one.

An awareness of how our culture subconsciously sets us up to orbit separate spheres helps us intentionally create front porch/public space moments in our lives. We can offer our families a chance to forge the vibrant relationships we've talked so much about together.

Let's consider three attitudes of a front porch life. You may already live by some of these ideals, but creating a separate file in your brain for this conversation is important: go outside, let go of the idols, be invitational.

1. Go Outside

In Chicago the weather is unpredictable and dramatic. It's not uncommon to swing over 40 degrees on the thermometer in just one day. It's also not uncommon to hide out for the entire month of February. Many moms can park their cars in an attached garage and go straight into the kitchen without breathing fresh air en route from the grocery store. And since today's homes are larger, offering more indoor play space than ever before, it is easy to miss opportunities to connect with others because we simply love to play in the basement.

"Go outside and play" was the constant command of my own mother. This forced us into an expanding world of playmates and connections for the whole family. It meant that we got to know the Helphrey family across the street, and later our parents became friends (who still vacation together to this day). It meant that our escapades down the street at Jenny and Laura's place brought my mom over to hang out with their mom, Carol. I still know Carol to this day and remember exactly how she likes her coffee (lots of cream and sugar).

According to the Kaiser Family Foundation, today one in four children under age two has a television in their bedroom and children under age six spend the same amount of time watching television as they do playing outside.[3] This is not a rant against TV since I can plop my kiddos down for *Curious*

George like everyone else. But those hours in front of a screen may also mean missed playmates and connections.

One easy way around this reality is to simply step outside. Take a bowl of grapes and stack of juice boxes outside to the front steps after school, wait to see who crops up in the neighborhood. Our particular street is short on children, so at times all we see are a few neighbors walking dogs. But at least we are present. This past winter in Chicago, we had one snowfall that was a record twenty-plus inches, and my neighbor called me up to see if the kids wanted to trudge down the street and flop around in her backyard for a bit. Snow angels down the street, yippee! Weather phenomena like this always draws people out to connect. Standing with hands on our hips, we marvel at whatever mischief nature conjured up. Whether felled branches from thunderstorms or five-foot snow drifts, people come out in chaos.

Sadly it often takes local drama to bring people together. Floods and storms make allies out of former strangers as neighbors lend help and tools to one another. Then the event passes and everyone heads back inside until the next disaster.

Getting outside will look different for each family depending on climate, neighborhood, and culture. Some need to find their outside time at a local park or recreation area, while many native Texans won't dare flop on the porch in 110-degree August heat (which makes total sense). Find at least one way to plop yourselves purposefully in the presence of others. For most moms, the best way to achieve this end will be heading outside a few minutes each day.

2. American Idols: Letting Go of Them

David Goetz, in his book *Death by Suburb*, made a statement about what we idolize that poked directly into my little soul. "We all end up competing for the same symbols," says Goetz. "The Pottery Barn colors . . . the fuel-guzzling truck, the purebred dog, the family pilgrimage to Disney World, and the athletic and scholarship-bedecked college-bound freshman. My wife says that she doesn't really covet her neighbor's husband but only the size 6 figure of his wife."[4] He goes on to unpack the consumer mentality that plagues our purchases and warns of the havoc this mantra plays on our lives. We have a competitive covetous side.

Do you struggle to keep up with those darn Joneses? We are tremendously blessed. Half of planet Earth does not have a house or even a comfortable bed. Most of us are well aware that millions clamor for food, medication, and the chance to go to school while we loaf around eating Wheat Thins. Yet have you ever hesitated to host a new friend or a soiree in your home because perhaps your space was not big or tidy enough?

For me this neurosis plays out when I consider hosting our neighborhood Bunco group—this matronly dice game that my grandmother would be proud I know how to play. Bunco is really more about twelve to sixteen women snacking and chatting for four hours than anything else. A troop of very welcoming women a few blocks over invited me into their Bunco circle and some of them live in phenomenal homes—ones with new furniture and decor that actually match, draperies that were custom-made to fit the windows, and sumptuous rugs three inches thick that nibble at my toes.

I'm panicked about my turn to host Bunco.

We moved into our place three years ago and are still short on furniture. Our kitchen cabinets are also dusty and crooked. I often say that you can eat off our floors . . . because there is enough food stuck there to fix up a nice plate for lunch. That, and my boys have bad aim, often missing the toilet in our guest bathroom.

I'm really the only one who cares about any of this.

The Bunco crowd is a very warm circle of women who will laugh and connect in a home with 3,000 square feet or 300. No one cares. Yet I still freak out about it.

Fears like this hinder our ability to have a front porch life. If we are not willing to invite people over or to open up space for potential friends, then what sort of rhythm are we creating? One of paranoia, a rhythm that presumes the thought patterns of others, a rhythm of competition and fear. Let's do the work to get over our penchant for comparison. Make the bold decision to care less about the stuff and connect better with the people. Your life is *not* the sum total of your stuff. We are told that *Keeping Up with the Kardashians* matters, but the real-life people we meet typically do not require us to keep up, just to be fully present, like make eye contact and actually care.

3. Be Invitational

When my oldest son started kindergarten last year, I found myself a nervous wreck. Not only was my baby sporting a new backpack and his first pair of Skechers, I was also entering a new world. If you have sent your first kindergartener off, you know the feeling. As we trudged up the street together, I watched my son bounce along completely giddy for this new adventure. And while the predictable "Oh, he's growing up so fast" tears slipped down my cheeks, I was shocked to find another set of tears sneaking out. Loneliness suddenly pulled a tsunami over me. Thank God for my enormous dark celebrity sunglasses.

The entrance was flooded with strangers snapping pictures and hugging, reconnecting after a summer apart. I watched as they kicked up easy conversations. It seemed as though the entire yard of parents knew one another, even the other kindergarten moms who technically should have been as lost as I was. We had just moved into the neighborhood. I hugged Charlie and watched as he bounded through the doors in search of new buddies while I wheeled the stroller around to schlep my lonely self, a toddler, and a nine-month-old back home.

The entire next week I woke with the same nervous ache in my gut and pushed that ridiculously heavy double stroller back up the block. Super embarrassing to admit all this, by the way. Then one happy Monday I finally saw the only other mom I knew, my old trusted friend Liz, a Bestie for sure. Standing in a circle of her neighbors, she met me smiling and waving, then offered me the most simple yet profound gift—she introduced me to her friends. I wanted to pounce on them and beg them to let me sit at their lunch table.

Perhaps you have found yourself in a similar situation and you know the power of a small gesture to make a huge difference in your lonely heart. I could now wave and nod to a whole three people on our walk to school and it was glorious! We've all felt the pain of being new or alone, like being at a seminar when you only have a sticky name tag and a stale cup of coffee with thirty minutes to kill before the lecture starts. So you pretend you need to go to the restroom, which kills all of five minutes, leaving you twenty-five minutes to either be uncomfortable or pretend to be engrossed in some random brochure. How the game changes once we discover a companion!

To live invitationally is to live with an eye toward connecting with others. It means we remember that while we may have connected lives, not everyone has that same treasure. Many of us moms are lonely, so reaching out from your place of abundance helps tremendously. A simple "Hey, have you met my friend Rebecca?" moment might help another mom keep her sunglasses from sliding off her face with the rest of her tears.

Invitational living recalls the hobbies and pastimes of others so that we can introduce the two moms who are training for their first 10K. It means we always have an open seat at the BBQ for that woman from Boston who just moved in down the block. It means we never, ever underestimate the power of a simple smile or playdate invitation, ever. Or of putting our hand on a shoulder and saying, “Hey you with the preschooler sporting the baseball glove, you look a little confused, can I help you figure out the T-ball program?” Some of the daily elements we take for granted can profoundly move another mom to a healthier place. To live invitationally is to view our daily routines as a way to create warmth where loneliness reigns.

FIVE Mom-Tested Tips

1. **Keep your fridge stocked.** Keep an ample supply of lemonade, Popsicles, juice on hand. Part of living invitationally is to be a gracious host (not Martha Stewart, just a person who stocked up last time she went to the grocer). Pile up cheap, welcoming goodies and offer the warm invitation to stop by. When I was a kid, we always flocked to the house with the best carbohydrates. Seriously, we knew where every Twinkie stash was on the block and we played at the houses with food. Consider what it could look like for you to be the home where people stop by and know they will be met with a juice box and friendly chatter.

2. **Ask for nearby help.** If you are heading out of town, ask a neighbor to manage your mail and trash cans or water your plants. Sure the USPS can hold your mail and your cousin can water your plants, but why not ask someone nearby? Most people find these sorts of tasks easy and it helps establish a relationship. And my experience has been that most people want to help and often look for ways they might offer assistance to others. These are easy ways to begin those partnerships. And then you owe them and can invite them over for dinner when you have time.

3. **Have an HGTV moment.** This sounds quite Ty Pennington or Candice Olson and please know that my husband and I don't have a dime

to remodel anything. But if we did, near the top of our list would be reclaiming part of our front porch. If you are remodeling or upgrading your living space, think through the statement your proposed change makes to your neighborhood. Can you keep or reclaim a front porch? Is your architecture inviting? Seriously reconsider a back deck if a front porch is an option for you.

4. **Host a driveway (or balcony, alley, sidewalk) event.** Last summer my neighbor Laura sent an email to the parents on our block and invited us down for ice cream one Saturday night. She dropped four gallons of ice cream, maraschino cherries, and chocolate syrup into a cooler and pulled it onto her driveway. Two hours later we were still chatting as sticky kids bolted across the lawn. A perfect way to end a summer day. Low cost. Low stress. High invitational value!

5. **Stick close to home.** Keep your life oriented around your community. Cut down on the time you spend driving across urban (and even rural) areas. If your library, doctors, dentist, dry cleaners, and favorite coffee shop are nearby, you will spend less time in your car and more time in your community. The recent cultural trend to shop and buy local dovetails nicely here. Support your local economy and neighbors by sticking closer to home and investing everything—from your relationships to your finances—just down the street. You will find yourself spending less time in the car and more time right in your neighborhood.

Thumbs UP Thumbs DOWN

Which ideas in this chapter are within my comfort zone to incorporate?

Which ideas in this chapter would unsettle me too deeply to incorporate at this time?

BOOKS, PEOPLE, and OTHER RANDOM STUFF

- David Goetz, *Death by Suburb: How to Keep the Suburbs from Killing Your Soul*
- David Brooks, *On Paradise Drive: How We Live Now (and Always Have) in the Future Tense*
- Skye Jethani, *The Divine Commodity: Discovering a Faith beyond Consumer Christianity*
- The Center for a New American Dream, http://www.newdream.org/
- Lorilee Craker, *Money Secrets of the Amish: Finding True Abundance in Simplicity, Sharing, and Saving*

Section Three

Sharing Your Rhythm

10

Hot Potato

Helping Others Find Their Groove

Most of all, love each other as if your life depended on it. Love makes up for practically anything. Be quick to give a meal to the hungry, a bed to the homeless—cheerfully. Be generous with the different things God gave you, passing them around so all get in on it: if words, let it be God's words; if help, let it be God's hearty help.

—from 1 Peter 4 Message

How wonderful it is that nobody need wait a single moment before starting to improve the world.

—Anne Frank

Your Own Rhythms

After achieving a certain level of pre-teen hula hooping prowess, my childhood playmates and I inevitably got bored and conjured up new tricks. The toughest was our attempt at taking over the hula once another girl had started spinning. Standing on the steamy August asphalt, one of us would fire up the hoop while another crawled toward her ankles. The plan was to slither up alongside our friend and somehow match her rhythm and take over spinning the hoop. I mostly recall tiny granules of pavement denting my kneecaps during this endeavor.

Needless to say there is not a YouTube video of our feat, as we never did manage to pass off the spin to another girl (that, and this was way before "Al Gore invented the internet"). But totally milking this metaphor, I do look back to find a winsome reminder that we absolutely must create our *own* distinct rhythm. For to try to sidle up under another person's hoop messes with your own groove.

The Sigh of Relief Sermon

Several years ago one of the pastors at my church preached a sermon that had me skipping out of the building like I'd lost twenty pounds and won U2 tickets all in the same moment. Reverend Daniel White (now a pastor in California—making him infinitely cooler than he already was) and his wife, Lisha, are two of the most thoughtful, grace-filled people that I know. They also totally live in reality with four children and all that comes from a house filled with little people.

Pastors have made an agonizing career choice that requires them to forever finesse and cajole ancient ideas in an attempt to spring us all to action every week. It's a job that often feels a bit like coaxing a first grader to put on his shoes. Every morning, same routine. You stress the importance of footwear and they look at you as if boots in January were completely optional and utterly boring. I imagine this is what it feels like to preach fifty-two Sundays a year. You fire up your passion and pour out your soul while hundreds of people stare and contemplate post-service brunch plans.

With this same passion for spurring others to action, Daniel preached it up good one Sunday by urging others to get involved in opportunities to serve—which made me wince and fake nod, like I was totally (not) fired up about this topic. "Yeah, yeah, I get it, help others, get off the couch, get out there, the world needs our efforts." Not exactly a news flash yet not exactly something we do either. Statistically speaking, most people stick to the sidelines of life. A recent MOPS survey performed by the Barna Research Group revealed that only 32 percent of MOPS participate in a service project outside of their home. But perhaps this is okay for a season?

The Pareto Principle is a widely known glimpse of this reality. It states that roughly 20 percent of the people involved in an effort bring about 80 percent of the outcome. This little tidbit came to mind as I listened to Daniel's sermon. As a representative of the slacking 80 percent, I agreed the world could use a few more volunteers, but I had no immediate plans to be one of them. I was eight weeks into life with a newborn, so who was I to be helping anyone else? But Daniel carried on, citing Bible verses and nudging us all toward the reality that God wants us involved in the world. I slid farther down into my pew. And then, as preachers love to do before they make a point, his voice changed and he got all quiet and contemplative. Here comes the zinger, right?

He switched it up and said the magic words my heart still celebrates: "And to the parents in this room who are the primary caregivers for their children, don't stress about this, for you are doing a tremendous job each and every day." He went on to acknowledge all the effort that goes into this life stage and to let us off the hook for volunteering to run the Jaycees Carnival, the next 4H event, and VBS as a result of his sermon.

He celebrated the fact that mothers are in the throes of changing lives every day, and if we can settle into that rhythm, we may ultimately add a few globally conscious children to the game—and that trumps any halfhearted, guilt-inspired service project with a three-month-old on your hip. Sitting out a few rounds of volunteer work might actually help this world! (Read that again.)

There are few pastors I have met who both understand and champion the lives and voices of parents and mothers the way Daniel did. So thankful! Know that the efforts you make every day just to keep babies fed and clothed may be all that this world asks of you . . . for now.

On the Other Hand . . .

Since this is an entire chapter devoted to getting involved, you knew there would be a catch. As life ebbs and flows, we come in and out of opportunities to offer our gifts and talents to those around us. The catch at this life stage is recognizing our investment in the world is not an all-or-nothing endeavor.

Open a food pantry or watch a *House Hunters* TV marathon? These are not the only two options.

Each day is ripe with some sort of possibility. Author and parent Katrina Kenison notes the recurring opportunities found in any ordinary afternoon: "Days in which we simply attend to the humble business of life—making meals and eating them, cleaning up afterward, doing algebra problems, practicing for next week's piano recital, paying bills, coming and going, until finally, at day's end, we are reunited for a little while, to share a laugh . . . the satisfaction of our togetherness."[1] Even the most mundane, seemingly benign effort, like a well-placed smile or family meal, adds positive energy and God's goodness to this world. Our invitation is to enter those moments regardless of the size and scope. This is how our world changes for the better, one small act of love and grace at a time.

"But I'm Just a Mom"

If we are indeed designed to love one another and move this world toward a better future, it sure helps to remind ourselves that (as my friend Laura Carlson Goetsch says) "Moms make the world go 'round." Women have been doing the work of enhancing human life for centuries. We're short on details to conjure up conversation about US involvement in NATO or Timothy Geithner's latest decision; many of us know far more about Leapster games. But whether pressing our local school for reading programs, fixing a meal for a new mom, or responding to a crisis in the community, moms are the first responders. The researchers, organizers, Band-Aid-toting, tear-wiping cheerleaders for life.

Yet our culture seems a bit confused as to how exactly to categorize moms. It both idealizes and limits the significance of motherhood. We tout its tremendous significance, claiming it as the highest call, as we simultaneously dismiss it in the marketplace. Ann Crittenden, a former economics reporter for the *New York Times*, wisely noticed that "a mother's work is not just invisible; it can become a handicap. Raising children may be the most important job in the world, but you can't put it on a resume."[2] Crittenden goes on to identify an experience many mothers encounter. "Any woman who has devoted herself to raising children has experienced the hollow praise that only thinly conceals smug dismissal. In a culture that measures worth and achievement almost solely in terms of money, the intensive work of rearing responsible adults counts for little. . . . How did the demanding job of rearing a modern child come to be trivialized as baby-sitting?"[3]

In other words, when sitting at a table of seemingly accomplished strangers at your second cousin's wedding, if you spend most of your time at home with kids, you may find yourself murmuring, "Please don't ask me what I do for a living, please let the topic change before it gets to me. That guy is an architect and she is a bond trader, I wash Onesies for a living."

When asked, "So what do you do for a living?" moms who spend part or all of their time at home with children often struggle for a response. I eavesdrop on this reply constantly. They throw in some sort of caveat. Personally, I've been one to choke here too. "Well, I *just* stay at home with the kids, so let's talk about you. That's so much more exciting." Or, "I work part-time but really *just* stay at home with the kids." *JUST* stay at home?!?! There is no *just* about it.

There is no paycheck attached to motherhood. Sure, the benefits are amazing. Midday hugs and conversations that fill our journals. But come Friday we don't get a check. No annual review. No assessment of progress, goal setting, or promotion. For all your work you eventually win a hormonal middle school child who bolts from your presence lest she seem utterly uncool.

Still, no such thing as *just* a mom.

Our days are spent shaping self-aware, confident contributors to society, yet our culture, combined with our own inability to celebrate this fact, keeps us wanting to say something flashy at that wedding reception. Maybe it even fuels a decision to volunteer or help out at a time that is completely wrong for our family. Why isn't "Well, I work really hard at shaping the souls of my children so that they become competent, wise contributors of society" enough? "I spend my days duking it out with the world so that my super-confident daughter can sit at this very table someday and tell you about how her own life is contributing to this world." Let this be enough! It will slow down your rhythm and help you live into the beautiful reality of your everyday work.

Not *just* a mom, but a world-changing, people-shaping, caring, life-giving woman swaying to a rhythm that can indeed change the trajectory of this very world. Dr. Martin Luther King Jr. and Susan B. Anthony had amazing moms. We do indeed make the world go 'round! So work it and own it. Make Tyra jealous.

Ancient Wisdom

There is an old tale found in both Turkish and Jewish folklore. It tells the story of the task a king (possibly King Solomon) gave to the captain of his guards. The captain was to find a ring with an inscription that could make both a rich man cry and a poor man rejoice. He traveled the countryside looking for this ring, wondering what sort of statement could bring those with lavish luxury to tears while picking the humble and needy up off the ground. A ring that offered both distress as well as comfort.

When the king's guard finally located this ring, he presented it to the king, conjuring up both a sigh and a groan from the king himself. The inscription was short; it read Gam Zeh Ya'avor.[4]

"This too shall pass."

Our parenting journey feels a bit like Jewish folklore. On the one hand we are so very eager for babies to sleep through the night, learn to walk, or give us a 2.5-hour break by heading to preschool—so eager for it all to pass. Yet never again will we snuggle all night with the heady scent of a newborn or cheer on first wobbly steps. Musician Sara Groves, in her song *Small Piece of You*, sings about eighteen years that go by like a blur.

I once asked speaker and consultant Mary Byers to help me navigate a writing career and motherhood. She sat me down and her opening line was actually quite ancient: "This will pass," she said. "It will get easier. You are in one of the hardest stages of parenting. It gets easier." To which I squealed, "I knew it! I knew it had to get better." Yet at the same time Mary warned me not to expect too much of myself at this point or I would miss so many God-given moments. To which I sighed, "I know it. I know it."

This too shall pass, right?

Don't rush it. Life accelerates on its own. The Girl Scouts and Bono will still need your help five years from now. By high school most kids are potty trained and no longer want to sit on your lap. Your ability to whisper blessings and prayers into their ears diminishes each year while their own attitude toward the world grows. Don't panic, but hold them tight, while you can. This too shall pass.

Embracing This Rhythm

Only by recognizing both the limits and abundance of this life stage can we discover any additional places we may be invited to contribute our time and energies. We hold Daniel's sermon notes in one hand while looking ahead for open space.

Eventually we will flop into a chair and find our exhaustion less than what it once was. We actually slept six hours last night!

One day you see another mother dragging tattered bags and wearing worn clothing who is short on cash to buy milk. She sleeps at the shelter across town, and suddenly you wonder if she needs any help. A sneaking suspicion arises in you that you may actually, finally be in a place to help. With timidity and anticipation you poke around to see what the needs are, still embracing your kids and your life stage, but suddenly aware that your value has *always* transcended your own home.

There will come a time when you can serve not out of guilt but out of abundance. Out of time well spent. Plans intentionally made. Remembering to rest wisely along the way.

Shani

My friend Shayne Moore sums it up well: "Our world is changing. Not all of us are called to huge activities outside our house, our town, our church—but all of us are called to do something. We have unprecedented access to each other, to ideas, and to resources." She goes on to say that she is not a politician, policy maker, preacher, or expert. She's a mom following God's call to fight for a better world.[5]

I confess that I've looked at Shani with envy. She goes to Africa what feels like every other week. She sits on the board of a few super-hip nonprofits that bring antiretroviral drugs to those with HIV/AIDS or equitable trade practices to coffee growers. Richard Stearns and Bono endorsed her book, and she once flew on a Learjet with Richard Branson and met Julia Roberts while doing advocacy work. If I met Julia Roberts, I would just end up quoting *Pretty Woman* to her while grinning like I was six.

When I sit in the same room with Shani, I can get all tangled up in myself. I suddenly feel the gravel from my hula hoop days pressing into my kneecaps once again. Only this time it reminds me that I will never, nor should I ever, try to spin another person's hoop; that I'm doing the very best work I know how to do each day; and that the life of my family will be one that impacts this world for good if I can just settle in and celebrate the rhythm of my own life as a mother.

I don't need to hop a Learjet with Julia, I just need to find my own rhythm and stay true to the way I know best how to serve.

FIVE Mom-Tested Tips

1. **Hug and a blessing.** Begin the habit of saying a blessing over your children at one point in the day when you hug and send them off (to school, to bed), recite a short one-sentence prayer that becomes your wish for the world through them. Simple, easy. Just whisper it to yourself first and later verbalize it to them. "May you bring peace to those around you." "May you bring light to this world." "May others find hope because of you." Fortune-cookie-sounding stuff, yet a powerful, rhythmic reminder for them to be blessed and to be a blessing.

2. **Encourage compassion and empathy.** If you indeed believe that it does not take a trip to Zambia to make a difference in this world, then begin to model that for your children. As your children grow, consider starting each day with a challenge for them to find one lost or lonely person along the way and simply smile or encourage that person—the kid from your T-ball team who can barely hit, the girl from dance class crying each week. Invite your children to look for these situations once a day and have them consider if a hug, smile, or simple hello might help another person they meet along the way.

3. **Brag.** Women typically struggle to boast about their accomplishments. Consider shamelessly bragging about your role as a mom. When asked "What you do all day?" smile and list out all the ways your daily routine shapes the hearts and

minds of your children. Flaunt your activities, bask in the joy of your multitasking prowess. Resist the urge to slump your shoulders or defend why you decided to become a mother. Act like you are the Steve Jobs of parenthood.

4. **Pray.** Take a moment to pray through the first half of chapter 3 from Ecclesiastes (an Old Testament book from the Bible, vv. 1–8):

Dear God, please help me to remember that

there is a time for everything,
and a season for every activity under the heavens:
a time to be born and a time to die,
a time to plant and a time to uproot,
a time to kill and a time to heal,
a time to tear down and a time to build,
a time to weep and a time to laugh,
a time to mourn and a time to dance,
a time to scatter stones and a time to gather them,
a time to embrace and a time to refrain from embracing,
a time to search and a time to give up,
a time to keep and a time to throw away,
a time to tear and a time to mend,
a time to be silent and a time to speak,
a time to love and a time to hate,
a time for war and a time for peace.

Please help me to find the right time for me, to discover your pace and to live your rhythm. Amen.

5. **Journal.** Take another look at our prayer from Ecclesiastes. What "time" resonates with you at the moment. Are you silent or speaking? Warring or finding peace? Weeping or dancing? Take a few moments to identify what season you are in as well as whether you are entering or leaving that season.

Thumbs UP Thumbs DOWN

How have you experienced the great joy and value of your efforts as a mom?

Where have you felt undervalued or overlooked because of your role as a mother?

BOOKS, PEOPLE, and OTHER RANDOM STUFF

- Adele Calhoun, *Invitations from God: Accepting God's Offer to Rest, Weep, Forgive, Wait, Remember, and More*
- Arloa Sutter, *The Invisible: What the Church Can Do to Find and Serve the Least of These*

11

Triple Dog Dare

Can We Really Live This Out?

And what happened then . . . ? Well . . . in Who-ville they say
That the Grinch's small heart grew three sizes that day!

—Dr. Seuss, from *How the Grinch Stole Christmas*

Our prayers for others flow more easily than those for ourselves. This shows we are made to live by charity.

—C. S. Lewis

Hitting Rock Bottom

A week after I sat down to start this book my world mostly imploded with the loss of my childhood friend Traci (the rock-star you met in chapter 8). I was on page 34 of this book. Then one drippy Monday morning on my way to work, I got another call from lifelong friend and neighbor, Liz. Her husband Joel had contracted meningitis and was in emergency brain surgery. The outlook was iffy at best.

Do you have a person in your life who is rock solid, there for you always, doesn't care if you forgot deodorant (mostly because they probably did too)? The kind of friend you both cry with and talk about bikini waxes with? Who would love you forever whether you wanted it that way or not? Liz is one of those people.

I sat on a tacky pastel chair in a hospital waiting room, watching one of my very best friends tremble at the thought of losing her husband and the father of her four- and seven-year-old children. The sallow fluorescent lighting cast everyone in a blue shadow—a fitting hue for the morning as I sat running my hands back and forth along the worn armrests. These gummy handles were gripped just yesterday by another family in this first wave of crisis. I wonder how it went for them? My heart silently began to scream, *Can this really be happening again?*

"Hey God, FYI, in case you had not noticed, these are good folks, parents with very young children. They still have things like the first day of kindergarten and freshman year coming down the pike. Could you ease up on my people, please? Just thought I would ask, since you are in the business of arranging these sorts of comings and goings."

Emergency rooms are surreal enclaves where hope, fear, panic, and desperation mingle like a cocktail party. And yet these are the places where friendships grow because they've wrestled with reality.

Those First Responder Moms

It quickly became clear this was no four-hour ER visit. I eavesdropped on Liz's family while helping her kids keep busy, filling small Dixie cups with coffee, sugar, powder creamer, and dust to make magic soup.

When was the last time anyone ate? Did she leave her back door unlocked? Did her colleagues at work know yet? How were the kids getting to school? It's only Monday. And who was going to whip up dinner while everyone just "waited to see"? They needed someone just one circle out. A mom. A friend. A woman who knew both her address and the routine at school. The gal who lived a few blocks over and knew her neighbors. A woman who was clued in on if they drank 2% or skim.

Ever sat through a moment like this? When you realize that the best option for help may just be you?

Wide Margins

The thing about finding your rhythm as a mom is that when crisis hits, when people need you, if you have been wise and willing with the cadence of your life, you have enough margin left over to help others. If your rhythm allows for it, you can step in and make a difference. Within two days we had an enormous team of parents doing everything from shuttling a Gold Mite to hockey practice to washing Liz's floors and doing her laundry.

Moms, it turns out, do indeed make the world go 'round.

If Only . . . Then I Could . . .

Have you ever tried to focus on a task when your heart felt like it had arthritis?

"If life would just stop happening to the people I love, then I could write this book about how to love people when life happens."

Wait. What?

Why discuss vibrant relationships if we cannot take the time to live them? One of my friends is a pastor and he often jokes that ministry would be easy if only the people would keep from getting in the way—how he could write a brilliant sermon if he did not have to sit at the bedside of a struggling church member. How clean might your kids' rooms be if they did not play there? Kidding of course, but hints of truth slip through in the joke.

You see, life is happening now. We can talk forever about the idea of finding our rhythm, of letting that rhythm guide our relationships, but for each one of us, eventually it comes time to dance.

When you finally do reach that point, will you be ready to jump in? And how exactly does one come out of the parenting fog and into the mess when life happens? Sometimes the game finds you. There are moments when all you have lived and discovered about yourself comes into focus. At times we have the luxury of sitting and dreaming; other times we just have to act.

Retrofit Your Daily Life

In his book *Seizing Your Divine Moment*, Erwin McManus tells the moving story of his ten-year-old son who leapt to action when he saw a double amputee fall from his crutches on a Florida beach. While adults, including McManus himself, looked on and weighed the personal cost of action, his son ran to this man's side and tried to pull him up. Only when the strength of a ten-year-old boy failed to help did the rest of the onlookers step in.

McManus replays both his own shame for not stepping in as a potential helper as well as the pride he felt for his son, who inspired participation from the other onlookers. His son, according to McManus, had seized initiative and found a "divine moment."[1]

Divine moments abound. Each day is oozing with opportunity. Each of us sees just our own sliver of the possibility in this world. What captures the heart of one woman never occurred to the other. But each of us has the opportunity every day to seize divine moments, to repurpose pain, to retrofit grace and compassion into whatever situation God lays at our feet.

This is what it means to finally and fully embrace your rhythm. It means you recognize your rhythm was not meant for just you to dance alone, but for you to dance with the world around you. It invites you to join a symphony of others rather than playing a solo.

Weekend Update

Lest I leave you hanging, Liz's husband Joel made a miraculous recovery. He worked hard. He fought. And their family will tell you that the tremendous love, prayers, support, cards, meals, hugs, and shared tears are what pulled them through. The divine moments of a small army.

And here is the "rest assured" catch—the help they received was not rocket science. One mom three doors down threw Liz's laundry in with hers. A colleague picked up a few extra hours. A neighbor grabbed orange juice while already at the store. A friend wrote an encouraging note after her kids went to bed. Another mom baked a double batch of cookies early one morning. This is how the rhythms of our lives swing together in crisis. This is how we begin to reach beyond ourselves into the world around us. Amen for the routines of women.

On the Way to Convention

Living this out is possible. Divine moments abound, even at O'Hare International Airport. Several years ago I hopped a plane from Chicago to a MOPS International Convention. Traveling to big events always cracks me up because you know 50 percent of the plane is filled with attendees, so we had a 747 bursting with moms getting away for a long weekend. Oh, the estrogen.

It took all of thirty seconds for my companions and me to realize we were surrounded by other escapees. We had introductions and new BFFs nailed before the flight attendants even went through that safety shtick you feel mildly guilty ignoring. Would that flimsy yellow life vest really work anyway?

In the middle seat behind us sat a mother and her six-month-old son. This gal was not en route to a weekend sans kids but was surrounded by moms who were. We mostly chatted around and over her for half the flight as she tried to woo her fussy child to sleep. She apologized if he was too loud for us, which is hysterical since we were pretty much middle school girls at a slumber party by this point.

Suddenly the mom next to her asked for a turn to help with the baby, shifting the entire in-flight entertainment from polite disregard to helpful in one grace-filled comment. I picked up the slack by flashing the warmest smile I could muster and said, "Hey, if there ever was a flight where it was okay for a kid to cry, this is it." Surely empathy would abound on a plane filled with mothers?

Yet as her son upped the volume, heads began to turn—a few nonchalant glances pretending to check on the lavatory status, then resting with a sprinkle of spite on our little posse. A few clearly agitated women threw down daggers. This mom was quite young, obviously traveling without the father. So add a little self-righteous eyebrow lifting. Part of me thought, "Get over yourself, you meanies. Do you honestly think she wants this baby to shriek all the way to Texas?"

Of course these are just conversations in my own head, because I am too chicken to take on a plane of staring women. And sadly, who was I to comment, since I could recall a few occasions where I was less than patient with my own tribe. Like if I am working and in a hurry and you are blocking the door to the coffee shop because your giant double stroller was not designed to fit through that size space. I will holler at you inside my head. As if I did not try the exact same maneuver a week earlier.

Moms can be the worst sort of enemy too. It's up to us to spread the love or squash it. With one squinted eye and an irritated huff, we can crush another woman. This power terrifies me.

Attitude Is the Beginning of Everything

Our attitude toward other moms is a great starting point for where to jump in. In the story of McManus's son, I am sure some of the onlookers that day thought, "Well, I'd help him but he should have known better than to come to the beach anyway." Pick your possible excuse. The boy did not weigh the cost, he leapt to action.

So maybe get started by just being nice, by viewing other moms as partners for the journey rather than competition or somehow less than you because they forgot a toddler's jacket on a cold afternoon. Pick your playground cliché—"Do unto others . . . ," "Love your neighbor . . ."

That flight reminded me that a paper-thin line kept us from blowing off this poor girl in the middle seat. Barely three hours into our escape, each one of us could have ignored her or subtly suggested with a glare that her child best simmer down. Yet one mom broke the barrier by offering to help. Turns out it may just have changed that girl's life.

You see, our new pal in 33D was a single mom on her way to Dallas to drop her son off with Grandma while the mom shipped off for her first assignment in the US Army. A single woman, an unexpected child, a long commitment. We passed her baby around and this girl began to cry, pouring out the details of her life.

We found ourselves all tangled up with her and our in-flight pretzels. She looked at her son, cried at how much it hurt her to love him, how she already could not wait to get back but was also a bit excited about her tour in the Army because life had not exactly afforded her much in the way of opportunity. She wiped one last tear on her sleeve and asked what we were all doing together. We told her about MOPS (MOPS.org), which just so happens to have a program for military moms. She wrote it all down. "I'm so glad I met you all," she said. "You have no idea how much you just helped me."

Now was that so hard?

Extending Near and Far

It is healthy to be connected to local issues as well as the general trajectory of the world. It is good to know how to help out at school but also what famine and struggle look like in Somalia or the Congo. A healthy way to strike this balance is to pick one local issue, as well as one global issue, you want to explore and work with. My fondness for the statement, "think locally, act globally" is that acting locally teaches us how to think and act globally. Get involved at home and abroad (without having to go abroad).

Here is a quick glimpse of one global issue that moms just like us can become involved with—an example of global passion and local action.

Sheryl WuDunn and Nikolas Kristoff wrote a life-changing book titled *Half the Sky: Turning Oppression into Opportunity for Women Worldwide*. As Pulitzer Prize–winning journalists, WuDunn and Kristoff relay their research and firsthand experiences with the plight of girls, women, and mothers around the world. Once I had a daughter, my passion for what women and girls face became the center of my own do-gooder desires.

As I play with my toddler daughter, I picture what she would face were she to live in a culture that abandoned babies like her just because of an X chromosome. Or a place that sold her into slavery or the sex trade because she was an extra mouth to feed, not as valuable in the fields as a burly brother. Kristoff and WuDunn drew the title of their book from a Chinese proverb that says "Women hold up half the sky." I believe this.

After devouring their book, I realized that as a mother, daughter, sister, friend—and as a woman—we all have a responsibility to bring light and hope to other women. Not that I don't think men deserve an equal dose of love and hope, they absolutely do! But my heart is drawn toward supporting women. There is something about the art of mothering a child that fuels my passion. When I hear of injury and pain inflicted on other mothers trying to love their kids—and desperately longing for help in this sacred calling—it makes my body ache and my hope becomes a bit desperate. It's my "holy discontent," as Bill Hybels would put it.

Moms helping other moms is a soul-shaping endeavor, and you can be a part of the movement that helps empower them. From a seat on an airplane to a brothel filled with teenagers in Thailand, there is a place for you.

Why Saying No Can Help You Say Yes

Lisa is a mother of four from our church who would make you smile the moment you met her. She's one of those people who is never stingy with a grin. I often ambush Lisa with ideas and plans like a caffeinated hyena. Lisa is also phenomenally wise with her time. With four kids and a marriage, she has both coördinated our entire MOPS program and stepped aside for a self-imposed sabbatical from it all. If you ask Lisa for help, she will not instantly yelp "yes." She pauses, and only if it works for her heart, her family, the rhythm of her life, will she leap.

I've watched Lisa reflect wisely. I've seen her say no to really good opportunities to help. She lives with the blissful reality that she was not called to help the entire planet, just her one small corner. Lisa takes her time deciding and will say no when she needs to, so that when she jumps in, you get all of her.

So as you hear this call to step into the game, I beg you to do it like Lisa. I'd tell you to call her for coffee and ask her how it is done, but she may pass if it does not honor her routine. She'd cheer you on, though. Big, bold, wise, sassy, grace-filled cheers.

Find your passion (chapter 4) and go.

FIVE Mom-Tested Tips

1. **Re-engage.** When I had my first child, I burrowed under the covers for a year. News stories made me cry. Heck, some random AT&T commercial kept making me cry. I could not bring myself to be aware of the world. Eventually you are ready to peek out and take some time to check up (from trustworthy sources) on the news of the day. Maybe all you can do is pray for those people in Japan or that missing girl, but you will find yourself keeping connected to the joy and sorrow of the world so that when an opportunity comes along to serve, you know how to recognize it. On many occasions I have heard moms laugh off the fact that they are "so far removed from the world at this point in their lives"—which I understand (and have lived), but at some point we've got to re-engage. The world needs us to know what reality looks like for the millions of people in need. Ignorance is not always bliss.

2. **Read.** Find the stories of mothers who are involved in their world. The list of women who consider themselves "just like us" is long. And sure, you may say, "Well, you are not at all 'just like me' because I did not write a book and you did." But the reality is that the burgeoning population of mommy bloggers and writers all started from at least one common starting point—they are

moms. Discover what they did in their community and what justice, care, love, and help looks like from another unique setting so you can be inspired. At the end of this chapter you will find a good resource list of moms eager for you to read up on their conversation.

3. **Child sponsorship.** Consider sponsoring a child in an impoverished part of the world. Compassion International and World Vision are great places to start. For around $40 a month you can offer a child clean water, food, and an education. If you can scrape together the cash, this is about as easy as it gets to make a difference. You contribute your funds (automatic withdrawal even) and then get your kids to write a letter every other month and voilà! And on the flip side another mom is grateful because you, little ole barely-getting-by you, have given her child life. LIFE! Read that again. For $40 a month you can shape the trajectory of an entire family through one child. Again, no such thing as "just a mom," eh?

4. **Prayer.** If picking an idea and jumping in all sounds good but you are just not ready yet, at least consider praying about where God is inviting you to partner with his work in this world. Pray for him to show you the next step. Confess your fears and your inadequacies (we all have them). And simply tell God you are not ready, then ask him to make ready your heart. "Lord, I am trembling, I am confused. I am not ready.

Please open me up to the places where you have called, led, and gifted me to help. And give me the guts to jump into the game." Then brace yourself. This, my friends, is a dangerous prayer.

5. **Journal.** Take some time to write about the people/situations you see that really mangle your heart. Some of us are desperate to help neglected children or women who are victims of domestic violence. Some lose sleep over the fears that pregnant teenagers face. Perhaps you cannot get the image of that starving child out of your mind? Take a few pages and write up a profile of the people who tug hardest at your heart. Where do they live? What are the issues they face? What are the possible joys in their lives? What do they need most? And what do you have to offer?

Thumbs UP Thumbs DOWN

What is one way I see myself able to help others in this life stage?

What is one way I can barely imagine helping another person at this time?

BOOKS, PEOPLE, and OTHER RANDOM STUFF

- Keri Wyatt Kent, *Simple Compassion: Devotions to Make a Difference in Your Neighborhood and World*
- Margot Starbuck, *Small Things with Great Love: Adventures in Loving Your Neighbor*
- Shayne Moore, *Global Soccer Mom: Changing the World Is Easier Than You Think*
- Helen Lee, *The Missional Mom: Living with Purpose at Home and in the World*
- My first book (insert smiley face here) *Green Mama: The Guilt-Free Guide to Saving the Planet*
- International Justice Mission, http://www.ijm.org/
- World Vision, http://www.worldvision.org
- Compassion International, http://www.compassion.com/
- Heifer International, http://www.heifer.org

12

Flannelgraph

The Rhythm of Faith

Are you tired? Worn out? Burned out on religion? Come to me. Get away with me and you'll recover your life. I'll show you how to take a real rest. Walk with me and work with me—watch how I do it. Learn the unforced rhythms of grace. I won't lay anything heavy or ill-fitting on you. Keep company with me and you'll learn to live freely and lightly.

—Jesus, from Matthew 11:28–30 Message

Faith is what we pray to find at the end of poems. It is the substance we hope for, the creative evidence of things not yet seen . . . that there is something to discover at the end of life's poem.

—Joy Sawyer, from *Dancing to the Heartbeat of Redemption*

Here Comes the Jesus Chapter

Perhaps you have been waiting for me to get to this point, or maybe you suddenly sense an ambush, a church service coming on. Kumbayah! Some of you love God and you do church and this conversation is easy for you.

Others of you, not so much.

Some of us have experienced the dark underbelly of Christianity without ever meeting the grace-filled God. Pick your horrible adjective: judgmental, mean-spirited, pushy, political, angry, narrow-minded, argumentative, obnoxious, ignorant. Yikes. Throughout history significant pain and even terror have been inflicted in the name of Jesus. Ever seen that bumper sticker, "Lord Jesus, save us from your followers!"

And yet, many of us have been on the receiving end of the life-changing adjectives like grace, compassion, charity, celebration, dignity, hope, love, peace, presence. We have walked through the doors of a church to find everything from three-bean salad at a potluck supper to an all-encompassing embrace for our depleted souls. Our time in church with God's people has served up the most delicious moments in our lives.

Saying you believe in God is sort of like announcing the name of your baby for the first time. You choose a name with great care and deliberation. You believe it fits perfectly and finally blurt it out at some big family dinner hoping that your relatives love it, that they sense the merit and history behind it, that they don't leave mumbling about why you would opt for such an odd moniker. And you pray the ruffian who bullied your uncle in sixth grade did not have the same name.

I saved this chapter on God for the end, but not to bait and switch you. Discussing faith is messy. Whenever someone asks if I am a Christian, my response is, "Well, why do you want to know?" If you describe a Christian with the horrible adjectives, then, "Mmmm, nope." The good adjectives? "Yes indeedy."

If what the apostle Paul says is true, that "in him we live and move and have our being" (Acts 17:28), then despite the bad press, Jesus really is the hope of the world. He is utterly captivating. John Calvin called this God's "irresistible grace," a pull that transcends beyond ourselves toward all that is magnificent, awe-inspiring, and beautiful. Are you nestled in the good adjectives?

The Ultimate Tambourine

One college evening I went to a hippie church. The worship leader passed out a tambourine and that shaky egg thing to the first student who grabbed for them, which, obnoxiously, would be me. Bob Dylan, move over.

Sometimes I think God is like a giant tambourine-playing hippie. God keeps time for us. He gently rocks the tambourine, softly moves the shaker. He sprinkles restorative ideals like hope and peace across our lives with the desire that they will move our souls to dance with him. He's not on the edge of the stage screaming into a microphone, but he is definitely leading the band.

Slowly, subtly, gracefully. Always in a perfect, measured beat. Joy Sawyer said God's rhythm reminds us that "hope is a relief, freeing us from the exhaustion of wheel-spinning striving. It [hope/faith] means we can discard our hurried time tables, both for others and ourselves. And instead we can be confident in the fact that God is at work in us, writing our life poems."[1]

God is writing your life's poem and he is keeping measured time, the ultimate Maestro.

Lute, Lyre, and Other Ancient Instruments

It is impossible to have rhythm without eventually connecting to the source of the music. Scripture is filled with God's songs, his creativity bursting into the world, rejoicing and lamenting all that is beautiful and terrifying about our lives.

The Bible's Old Testament was written in ancient Hebrew. The Hebrew word *psalm* has a root that means "to pluck." So the book of Psalms is a compilation of poems that were meant to be accompanied by perhaps the harp or lute—songs intended for the soul. Listen to these rhythms:

> King David declared that "The earth is the Lord's and everything in it." (Psalm 24:1)
>
> "The heavens declare the glory of God; the skies proclaim the work of his hands." (Psalm 19:1)
>
> "For you created my inmost being; you knit me together in my mother's womb. I praise you because I am fearfully and wonderfully made; your works are wonderful, I know that full well." (Psalm 139:13–14)
>
> "Let them praise his name with dancing and make music to him with timbrel and harp." (Psalm 149:3)

A musician calling out to all who will listen and join the melody.

God Is with You as a Mom

God is cheering us on from the park benches of motherhood. He cares deeply about our sleepless nights, panicky hearts, decisions to go back to work or stay at home. God enlivens us as we discover his dreams for our families. I burst through the doors of my home church each week to swap hugs and eat donuts with a savvy, soulful group of moms.

When asked about God's investment in their parenting, here is what they shared:

Jen K. (five kids, blended family): "I see God in the precious things my kids say throughout the day. Their words are so pure, simple, unaffected, and unfiltered, which reminds me how as adults at times we are so far from reality."

Nancy C. (four kids): "During my busiest baby years God was mostly a service call when times were tough. I love getting older and giving up a few cares of this world to know that what really matters is God's purpose for me here on earth and the people he has placed in my life."

Sally C. (two adopted kids): "I spend a lot of time asking God to forgive me for all of my not-so-lovely mom moments. This may sound strange, but I have become more broken as a mom, and that brokenness has forced me to turn to Jesus. He uses motherhood (a source of joy and great frustration) to draw me closer."

Ivanna P. (five kids): "When I had five kids all five years and under, I had many moments of crying out to God for help. At the time I didn't feel like I was making it, but looking back now, only two years ago, I can't believe that I survived. I remember God helped me through."

Lisa M. (three kids): "I try to think about how big God's love for us is as I love and parent my kids. I'm not as gracious a parent as he is . . . that usually keeps me in tune with God."

Susan E. (three kiddos): "You can't control everything your child does. You can encourage, love, and guide them. Just like God does with us."

God crafted your very heart and soul, and those of your beloved children. He knows exactly how to help you recover from your parenting pitfalls and how to guide you through the long journey of raising your children. Pause for a moment and ask yourself how you might answer the same question. What is God teaching you as a mom?

A God Who Lives in Community

Because God is three in one (Father, Son and Holy Spirit), then the very core, the very essence of God is community. Three communing together as one. Swirling, twirling, existing together. (Explaining the Trinity is perhaps one of the most profound theological conundrums of all time, so rest easy if you find yourself going, "Enh, I don't get it.") From the Genesis moment when God formed the world until the last shred of sunlight beams across the planet, God will always will be one. Community forever. We read in the Creation story that all people are made in God's image, in the very likeness of God. So, if we are made in God's image, then in the very root of our DNA, we are wired for community.

Introvert and extrovert. Quiet and shy, chatty and gregarious. Lonely or chummy. Depressed, isolated, excited, irritable, exhausted, rejuvenated, energized, and reflective. Urban, suburban, or rural, we all, every single one of us, need other people to survive.

This is ultimately why vibrant relationships matter. They reflect and honor the divine. In community we find help and hope, we experience the true tenacity of faith. We catch a glimpse of God. Motherhood is like this at the deepest level—a divine dance with God, with your family. A chance to shift and bend, to merge and to twirl with the artist who crafted your soul so that you in turn can dance with others. So throw your head back and spin.

Holy Ground

What is your dance with God like? It is okay to doubt and question and wonder. Faith is not an exact science—it is a conversation, a relationship. The holiness of God upstages church attendance or starchy dress clothes. It transcends war and racism; it fights for justice and shines light into the deepest places of sadness and pain.

What do you believe about God?

A journey of faith begins at your kitchen table or on the playroom floor. God does not suggest we pretty up our lives and find some mountaintop to pray upon. He asks that we listen to the still, small voice calling in the midst of motherhood. Amid the cacophony of life, when you listen closely, you can hear it . . .

like when your child races past you, pulling along that slight breeze which follows their activity and for once you pause before hollering "slow down!"
and you catch a whiff of baby shampoo and sweat wafting past you.
and then you smile. deeply.
you're in the middle of your kitchen and suddenly you find it is holy ground.
you are face-to-face with the love, the God of the universe.
via a two-year-old.

Moses found his holy ground near a bush in a dusty climate. A bush. Not exactly the panorama most associated with the grandeur of religion. And just like Moses, we find God in dusty, cracker-crumbly places like this. So what will you do with your God moments? Will you take your heart and mind and rest them into the hands of God to follow along with Jesus? Sit back and recognize the Almighty has tapped out a heartbeat for the universe. That rhythm includes these messages:

You are loved,
the beloved of God.

You have a role to play,
love to give, and grace to receive.

Will you get up and dance? Faith, doubt, anger, fear, pain, joy, hope, eternity, grace—you can figure all those out later. All God wants is for you to join the divine rhythm. And I hope you do. Because the most vibrant relationship of all is the one you create with God.

I'm In! Now What?

In lieu of our fabulous "Mom-Tested Tips," I'd like to offer a few thoughts on faith. Many of you have found this chapter a nice reminder of what you already know. For those of you who feel yourself engaging in this conversation for the very first time in your lives, it helps to paint a picture of the divine dance of faith and follow that up with some creative ways to move forward.

FIVE Thoughts on Faith

1. **Find a safe person with whom to chat about faith and God**—a friend, spiritual director, or pastor who is wise and discerning. I urge you to find someone knowledgeable and safe. Ask your MOPS leader who she might recommend you chat with—perhaps it is her? Not familiar with MOPS? Click here: MOPS.org. Check out a few local churches in your area, get a sense of who is thoughtful and safe, and give a worship service a shot.

2. **Silence.** Find the quietest space in your house, lock yourself in a closet, wake up at 2:00 a.m. and sit out on your back deck—whatever it takes to catch a moment of stillness. Then sit back and listen. So often if feels like we need to chat it up with God, to apologize, confess, beg, or just yammer away. Force yourself to just listen. To start by simply praying, "Dear God, I am listening to you. Speak to me." And no, a voice will not likely ring out from heaven (but then again . . .). But you will begin the process of orienting your soul toward the peace and abundance of God. Just sit and be, sense and feel God.

3. **Read a Bible.** This is God's book, the words and stories, the chaos and drama he wanted us to know about. Take some time to pick up a copy if you do not have one. I recommend the New International Version or *The Message* paraphrase by Eugene Peterson. Start at the beginning with

the Creation story in Genesis or consider skipping to the New Testament and starting with the book of John. P.S.—The Bible is a story of real life, so don't expect perfect people or blameless saints to adorn each page. What you will see throughout is God's relentless passion for justice and love, for grace and mercy to transcend this world, in spite of our every human weakness.

4. **Pray.** Take time to offer prayers to God, beyond the shotgun prayers we fire off when late for a meeting or waiting for a medical diagnosis to go our way. Offer the following to God: *praises* for all the good and beauty you see, *confession* for all the ways you struggle, *thanksgiving* for all the abundance you personally have received, and *blessings* that you ask God to shower upon other people. Pray for how you hope God meets the needs and desires of your own heart as well as those you love both at home and around the world.

5. **Journal.** Consider a thankfulness journal. Keep track of all the ways you have been blessed that day. From a summer rainstorm to the fact that you have access to ibuprofen when you have a headache. From your children to your mail carrier. Each day is dripping with divine moments and our job is to take notice and to give thanks, to remember our place in the universe is one of humility and thanksgiving. Try to keep a list of ten things you are thankful for that very day. And consider creating a new list every day for one week. At the end reread your list and consider how a deeper awareness of the gifts in this world have shaped you.

Thumbs UP Thumbs DOWN

What is one conversation/question about faith and God that I am excited to explore?

____

____

____

What is one conversation/question about faith and God that I am scared or nervous to ask?

____

____

____

BOOKS, PEOPLE, and OTHER RANDOM STUFF

- Francis Chan's bestselling *Crazy Love: Overwhelmed by a Relentless God*
- John Ortberg, *God Is Closer Than You Think: This Can Be the Greatest Moment of Your Life Because This Moment Is the Place Where You Can Meet God*
- Jodie Berndt, *Praying the Scriptures for Your Children*
- Lauren Winner, *Girl Meets God: On the Path to a Spiritual Life*
- Online Bible in multiple languages and versions, http://biblegateway.com
- Soul Care Resources, http://www.soulcare.com
- Mindy Caliguire, *Spiritual Friendship*

Conclusion

Ever have one of those moments when your age, the fact that you are no longer sixteen, throws itself in your face? In my mind I am tan, thin, and barely a day over twenty-two. In reality, not so much. At church, lounging in a circle with four high school girls, I chatted it up about boys, fashion, gum, and all things dramatic, adolescent. It was midsummer, just a few years ago, and this pile of gals was also making plans for their big day at the beach later that week. I was their youth leader. I felt cool.

When their chatter turned to savage tans and tanning oil the suburban, overprotective, terribly uncool mom in me kicked in. "Girls, be sure to wear your sunblock or someday you will end up with all these age spots like me." My earnest, once-filled-with-freckles face smiled at them, hoping they would listen to my SPF campaign.

A smart, chatty gal named Meredith piped up, "Hey, we will be okay. I never even noticed your freckles before. And anyway, those wrinkles around your eyes make you look wise."

"WRINKLES?! Where, what wrinkles? Crow's-feet? Dear God, do I have crow's-feet already?"

I contemplated a dash to the restroom to inspect these reported creases.

"What did that commercial say about Retinol A?"

I sighed and just laughed. I did not know I had wrinkles around my eyes. You see your face every day. Cell by cell, age takes over, but slowly. Hair changes, freckles blend, lines appear. "Yeah, I guess I am not a high school kid anymore."

Once I calmed my little forever-desiring-youth soul down, I realized that Meredith had paid me a compliment. I somehow seemed wise to her. Somehow my life, my stories, they were impressive to her. In *The Message* paraphrase of Psalm 90:12, Moses asks God, "Help us live well. Help us to live wisely and well." Is this what Meredith saw? Lines of life well lived?

As games and shenanigans of our youth give way to diaper bags, rent, mortgages, oil changes, and grocery bills, we find fewer lemonade-filled summer days. But along the way we also find that the rhythm of our lives has afforded us some lessons. It leaves a little residue of wisdom that layers over all that we do. Taking time to develop relationships, to encourage and support others, to risk and grow and get involved, grants us the blessings of wisdom.

So as you find yourself in the throes of your own hula hoops, of finding space to move and breathe, of keeping up with the carpool while calming the calendar, I hope you find that your life is filled with a rhythm and cadence from God. As those wrinkles inch up your face, as those children inch up the growth chart, I hope you can settle into a swing that honors your dreams, your family's needs, and God's design for you. And I hope you still find time to go sledding or play Bingo, to chew a giant piece of bubble gum or sift bubbles through the air. Let the carefree routines of youth inform your life today.

Ultimately, when we live wisely, in time we discover how to connect vibrantly to one another in that time. And our *Mom Connection* deepens. Our days are metered, our pace is manageable. Mom connections are around us every day. We just need to open up our lives and step into them.

Notes

Introduction

1. Dorothy C. Bass, *Receiving the Day: Christian Practices for Opening the Gift of Time* (San Francisco: Jossey-Bass, 2000), 103–4.

Chapter 1 Hula Hoops

1. Hula Hoop World Records, http://www.recordholders.org/en/list/hulahoop.html.

2. http://www.youtube.com/watch?v=ePgSznNviO0.

Chapter 2 Teeter-Totter

1. Michele Borba, *Lonely Mom? Try Starting a "Momtourage,"* http://today.msnbc.msn.com/id/25689978/ns/today-parenting/.

2. *Building Strong Familes*, no. 5, March 2003, http://www.search-institute.org/system/files/SocialSupportforParents.pdf.

3. Adele Calhoun, *Invitations from God: Accepting God's Offer to Rest, Weep, Forgive, Wait, Remember, and More* (Downers Grove, IL: InterVarsity, 2011), 9.

Chapter 3 Two or More Players

1. Anne Taintor, artist/author.

2. Jean Blackmer, *MomSense: A Common-Sense Guide to Confident Mothering* (Grand Rapids: Revell, 2011), 66.

Chapter 4 Hide-and-Seek

1. "Chore Wars: Men, Women and Housework," National Science Foundation, http://www.nsf.gov/discoveries/disc_images.jsp?cntn_id=111458&org=NSF.

2. Louann Brizendine, *The Female Brain* (New York: Broadway Books, 2006), 100.

3. Ibid., 97.

4. Centers for Disease Control and Prevention, http://www.cdc.gov/nchs/data/databriefs/db21.pdf.

5. Brizendine, *Female Brain*, 96.

6. Caryn Dahlstrand Rivadeneira, *Mama's Got a Fake ID: How to Reveal the Real You Behind All That Mom* (Colorado Springs: WaterBrook, 2009).

7. Bill Hybels, *Holy Discontent* (Grand Rapids: Zondervan, 2007).

Chapter 5 Game Night

1. Andy Crouch, speaker, "The Disciplines for Surviving: Thriving in a Creative Calling," Synergy 2011 conference, March 5, 2011.

2. Jennifer C. Grant, personal interview with author, April 2011.

3. Adele A. Calhoun, *Spiritual Disciplines Handbook: Practices That Transform Us* (Downers Grove, IL: InterVarsity, 2005), 36.

4. Pete Scazzero, "The Rule of Life" worksheet, Willow Creek Transformation Intensive, May 5, 2011.

Chapter 6 Pinochle and Bingo

1. Erma Bombeck, *Family—The Ties That Bind . . . and Gag!* (New York: Random House, 1987), 11.

2. Judith Viorst, *Grown-Up Marriage: What We Know, Wish We Had Known, and Still Need to Know about Being Married* (New York: Free Press, 2003), 55.

3. Henry Cloud and John Townsend, *Boundaries with Kids: When to Say Yes, When to Say No, to Help Your Children Gain Control of Their Lives* (Grand Rapids: Zondervan, 2001).

4. Juliet Schor, *The Overworked American: The Unexpected Decline of Leisure* (New York: Basic Books, 1993).

Chapter 7 Ring Toss

1. Trisha Ashworth and Amy Nobile, *I'd Trade My Husband for a Housekeeper: Love Your Marriage After the Baby Carriage* (San Francisco: Chronicle Books, 2009).

2. "Single-Parent Households Showed Little Variation Since 1994, Census Bureau Reports," US Census Bureau, March 27, 2007, http://www.census.gov/newsroom/releases/archives/families_households/cb07-46.html.

3. David Code, *To Raise Happy Kids, Put Your Marriage First* (New York: Crossroad Publishing, 2009).

4. Wendy Cox, "The best thing you can do for your kids? Put your marriage first: author," interview with David Code, parentcentral.ca, May 18, 2010, http://www.parentcentral.ca/parent/newsfeatures/article/811019--the-best-thing-you-can-do-for-your-kids-put-your-marriage-first-author.

5. Wendy Edelstein, "When a Couple Become Collaborators: Psychologists Philip and Carolyn Pape Cowan on Their 30-plus Years of Partnership," *UC Berkeley News*, April 27, 2005, http://berkeley.edu/news/berkeleyan/2005/04/27_cowan.shtml.

6. Ibid.

Chapter 8 Telephone

1. Ellen Goodman and Patricia O'Brien, *I Know Just What You Mean: The Power of Friendship in Women's Lives* (New York: Simon & Schuster, 2000), 35.

2. Randy Frazee, Oak Brook Conference on Ministry, live presentation, November 2007.

3. John T. Cacioppo, James H. Fowler, and Nicholas A. Christakis, "Alone in the Crowd: The Structure and Spread of Loneliness in a Large Social Network," *Journal of Personality and Social Psychology*, 97, no. 6 (2009): 978, http://jhfowler.ucsd.edu/alone_in_the_crowd.pdf.

4. Clea Hantman, *30 Days to Finding and Keeping Sassy Sidekicks and BFFs: A Friendship Field Guide* (New York: Delacorte Press, 2009), 80.

5. Ibid., 81.

6. Rivadeneira, *Mama's Got a Fake ID*, 179.

7. Teresa Strasser, "Mom Profiling Is an Imperfect Science, but I Know Who You Are," Huff Post Comedy, *Huffington Post*, June 14, 2011, http://tinyurl.com/3qgdvr5.

8. Rosalind Wiseman, "Queen Bee Moms & Kingpin Dads: Author Talks about New Book," *Washington Post*, March 29, 2006, http://www.washingtonpost.com/wp-dyn/content/discussion/2006/03/23/DI2006032300970_pf.html.

Chapter 9 Hopscotch

1. Margot Adler, "Behind the Ever-Expanding American Dream House," NPR, July 4, 2006, http://www.npr.org/templates/story/story.php?storyId=5525283.

2. Jennifer Bradley and Bruce Katz, "A Small-town or Metro Nation?" Brookings Institution, October 8, 2008, http://www.brookings.edu/articles/2008/1008_smalltowns_katz.aspx.

3. "New Study Finds Children Age Zero to Six Spend as Much Time with TV, Computers and Video Games as Playing Outside," Kaiser Family Foundation, http://www.kff.org/entmedia/entmedia102803nr.cfm.

4. David Goetz, *Death by Suburb: How to Keep the Suburbs from Killing Your Soul* (New York: HarperOne, 2006), 65–66.

Chapter 10 Hot Potato

1. Katrina Kenison, *The Gift of an Ordinary Day: A Mother's Memoir* (New York: Springboard Press, 2009), 264.

2. Ann Crittenden, *The Price of Motherhood: Why the Most Important Job in the World Is Still the Least Valued* (New York: Metropolitan Books, 2001), 3.

3. Ibid., 45.

4. Heather Frost, *Wisdom Tales from Around the World* (Little Rock: August House, 1996), 72.

5. Shayne Moore, *Global Soccer Mom: Changing the World Is Easier Than You Think* (Grand Rapids: Zondervan, 2011), 15.

Chapter 11 Triple Dog Dare

1. Erwin McManus, *Seizing Your Divine Moment* (Nashville: Thomas Nelson, 2002), 33.

Chapter 12 Flannelgraph

1. Joy Sawyer, *Dancing to the Heartbeat of Redemption: The Creative Process of Spiritual Growth* (Downers Grove, IL: InterVarsity, 2000), 72.

Gracias

Friends. The kind who instinctively splash just the right amount of cream in your coffee. The stories on these pages come from those women. Beautiful souls from whom I learn so much.

Like Amy, Nancy, and Suanne who let me yammer away endlessly about my dreams and projects. Parenting comrades like Jana, Lisa, and Christine and women like Constance who will endure a day at the water park to love on my kids. Companions like Liz ("the sister I choose"), Donna, Laura, Jenny, and my sister Nikki who, through tragedy, know what the word *neighbor* really means. And new neighbor pals like Robin, Sonia, Rebecca, Joanna, Laura, and all the moms who warmly chat it up at school. Women like "Toast" who nudge lovingly toward better friendship. And for the women at Christ Church of Oak Brook whose voices and stories are scattered across these pages. You ladies inspire me deeply. And of course, Adele Calhoun, who helped me find my voice and settle my soul.

And my own Mom whom I love so deeply and my awesome mother-in-law who help my family raise up kids with love and grace. Thank you to my immediate family, Danny, Charlie, and Lilly—Mama loves you. And to Joel, thank you for once again watching me fret, fumble, ingest coffee, and twirl around in circles. Thank you for loving me well so these words could tumble forth. They would not be without you.

Thank you to the wise women at MOPS International, especially Carla and Jean for their continued encouragement of my voice, and to Elisa Morgan for launching me into MOPS. Thanks to my editor Andrea Doering for your help and that great breakfast last year. And a big shout-out to the Redbud Writers Guild (http://redbudwritersguild.com). A cacophony of faith, estrogen, dreams, ideas, voices, and the audacity to write it all down.

And finally, for Traci Boers. Where words fail, memories begin. You are forever on the driveway of my youth with a bathing suit, Popsicle, and a soul-shaping giggle. This book is for you.

Tracey Bianchi is the author of *Green Mama* and has been an active speaker, writer, and participant with MOPS for over seven years. She has three young children, a fabulous husband, and a goldfish named Stinky Pete. They live in the Chicago area, where Tracey serves as a ministry leader at Christ Church of Oak Brook and maintains a freelance career that includes speaking and writing for a wide variety of organizations. She earned her MDiv from Denver Seminary and needs a ton of coffee to make all of this work.

TRACEY BIANCHI
mom connection
creating vibrant relationships in the midst of motherhood
mom connection
BIANCHI

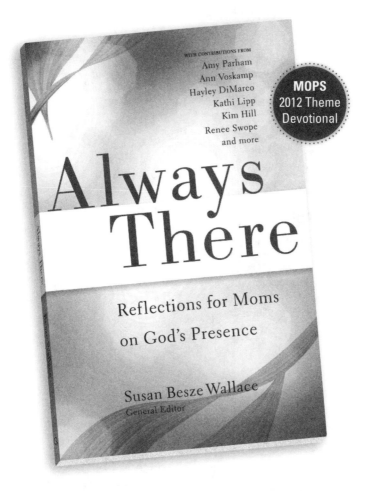

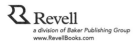